Also by W. Scott Moore

*Dead Ends or Destiny?
Seven Paths through the
Wilderness Experiences of Life*

*Exit Wounds:
Healing from the Hurts of the Ministry*

*Rural Pastor's Handbook:
A How to Guide for Leading Your Flock*

*Rural Revival:
Growing Churches in Shrinking Communities*

*Supernatural Strategy:
Discovering the Lost Key to Effective Evangelism*

*Uganda's Messianic Muslim:
How Jesus Christ is Transforming
the Life and Ministry of Nassan Ibrahim*

PARTNERS IN PLANTING

Starting and Staffing a New Testament Church

W. Scott Moore

Rogersville, Alabama

First Edition

Partners in Planting

Author: W. Scott Moore, B.B.A, M. Div., D. Min.
© 2012 by Eleos Press www.eleospress.com

All rights reserved.

This book or parts thereof may not be reproduced in any form, stored in a retrieval system, or transmitted in any form by any means without prior written permission of the author, except as provided by United States of America copyright law.

Cover Art: W. Scott Moore
Cover Design: W. Scott Moore
Interior Formatting: Eleos Press www.eleospress.com

Also available in eBook form

Unless otherwise noted, all "Scripture quotations taken from the New American Standard Bible®, Copyright © 1960, 1962, 1963, 1968, 1971, 1972, 1973, 1975, 1977, 1995 by The Lockman Foundation. Used by permission." (www.Lockman.org)

Eleos Press publishes this volume as a document of critical, theological, historical, and/or literary significance and does not necessarily endorse or promote all the views or statements made herein, or verify the accuracy of any statements made by the Author. References to persons or incidents herein may have been changed to protect the identity of those involved.

ISBN-13: 978-0615593487

PRINTED IN THE UNITED STATES OF AMERICA

Foreword

We live in a world of constant change. Americans even elected our 44th President basically upon his campaign promise to bring about so-called "change." And, agreeably, some things need to be changed. As a great scholar once quipped, "The babies in the nursery aren't the only ones that need changing!"

It's a fact, the world is constantly changing, people are changing and even churches are changing. Some churches change their names. Others change their locations. Some change their services times. And many churches even change their pastors! My dear friend, Scott Moore was one of those pastors. In a situation where ones first reaction would have most likely been "tragic," God has mercifully used Scott Moore's trial of being "let go" as a senior pastor, to blossom him into a prolific writer and church planter! (Romans 8:28 comes to mind!)

In Scott Moore's new book, "Partners in Planting," Scott cleverly grants us a unique glimpse inside the realms of successfully planning, organizing, and structuring a new church plant. Scott Moore takes us on his personal journey as an unemployed church pastor, to an adventurous path of becoming a modern day church planter. The reader will greatly enjoy the unique style of wit and conversation which are portrayed in this interesting book!

Whether you're the pastor of a growing, vibrant church, or barely surviving in a dying church, this book is a must read in exploring the options of growing God's kingdom work through church planting! As a senior pastor who just recently launched a new church plant and in the process of starting another church plant in a major city, I have personally gleaned many insights through reading Scott Moore's book, "Partners in Planting."

I highly recommend this insightful tool for every pastor, staff, elder, or church member who may, one day, become personally involved as a "partner in planting" a successful church.

> Dusty McLemore, Senior Pastor
> Lindsay Lane Baptist Church
> Athens, Alabama

What Others Have Said

Partners in Planting is Scott Moore's latest book in encouraging Christians to become followers of the commands of Christ. Moore is becoming one of the most prolific writers in the Christian market today. Read this book and apply its truths to your life.

> Carolyn Tomlin, co-founder and teacher of the "Boot Camp for Christian Writers" and author of the new eBook series, <u>What I Wish I'd Known Sooner</u>.

Scott Moore offers an innovative strategy for church ministry. Scott writes from his many years of ministerial experience.

> Eddy Garner, Director of Missions
> Colbert-Lauderdale Baptist Association
> Sheffield, AL

Scott Moore tells this story through his real-life experiences, and gives insight from his journey as pastor to layman and back to serving in a much different role. He brings great insight into how the church and its leadership must expand their thinking to be able to grow God's Kingdom and avoid unmet expectations from their local congregations.

> Jim Boyachek, Marketing Manager
> T.N.T. Fireworks
> Florence, AL

This book is dedicated to:
-My wife, Diane.
-And to our wonderful Lord and Savior, Jesus Christ.
He has faithfully led us on our adventure together as husband and wife for 40 years.

CONTENTS

INTRODUCTION i

Cast of Characters iii

The Return of Sam 2

Steve's Church 3

Meeting with Steve 6

The Pastors' Conference 9

The Interlude 16

Riverside Church 18

A New Beginning for a Church 41

Training Barnabas and Saul 44

Barnabas 60

Saul 94

The Formation of a Partnership 114

The Ministry Team 146

Start Date 154

Appendix: "A Composite Model" 159

Assembly Line Approach 160

Team Ministry 169

A Composite Ministry 176

CONCLUSION 185

INTRODUCTION

Why are so many churches unhappy with their pastors? And why are so many pastors unhappy with their churches? An old joke explains why: "A husband and wife went to see a marriage counselor; he asked them, 'Are you incompatible?' The husband, totally misunderstanding the question replied, 'My income's not so good, but she's not too *patable* either!'"

The obvious answer to the difficulties encountered in many pastor-church conflicts is that they are incompatible. And no amount of money on the part of the church, or catering on the part of the pastor, will ever change either the church or the pastor. They may make concessions and tolerate each other, but neither the members of the church nor the pastor will have the joy that God intended for them.

For this reason, placing a "Barnabas"[1] pastor into a "Saul"[2] church can be devastating to both. Similarly, placing a "Saul" pastor into a "Barnabas" church can be just as destructive.

---

[1] Those focused on *being*; relationally based.
[2] Those focused on *doing*; performance based.

But what would happen if you formed a co-pastoral team consisting of a Spirit-filled "Barnabas" and a Spirit-filled "Saul?" Could the two polar opposites coexist? Can they effectively work together to start and staff a New Testament church? God thinks so. He said in Acts 13:2: "Set apart for me Barnabas and Saul for the work to which I have called them."

Join Pastor Sam Anderson (Barnabas) and businessman Todd Williams (Saul) as they answer these and many other questions.

Cast of Characters

Rebecca Anderson — wife of Samuel

Samuel Anderson — former pastor of First Church

Sarah Caldwell — wife of Steve Caldwell

Steve Caldwell — pastor of Trinity Church

Carl Edwards — pastor of Unity Church

David Hanson — pastor of New Wine Church

Mike Jackson — pastor of Faith Church and program chairman for the Pastors' Conference

Ben Gilbert — director of the denominational association

Lee Thompson — pastor of Riverside Church

Todd Williams — businessman and former member of First Church

Lisa Williams — wife of Todd Williams

A New Beginning for a Pastor

There seems to be some debate over the origin of the phrase, "'It ain't over til' the fat lady sings." Wiki Answers lists three possibilities:[3]

1. *Opera— the "fat lady" refers to the strongest female diva [that] was often large; many popular opera end with an aria, or solo, by this singer.*

2. *Southern Sayings— there is a popular saying from the US Deep South from about the same time as the sports saying— this one says "Church ain't over 'til the fat lady sings," and refers to a member of the*

---

[3] http://wiki.answers.com/Q/Where_did_the_expr--ession_%27It_ain%27t_over_til%27_the_fat_lady_sings%27_originate, site -visited on 6-7-2011.

> *church choir, which is often composed of several large ladies.*
>
> 3. *An actual "fat lady" — Kate Smith was a large woman who was very popular as a singer in the 1930s to 1950s (Irving Berlin wrote God Bless America for her); in the 1950s, Kate had her own TV show, which ended right before the station went off the air for the night — thus, the TV broadcast day was not over until this particular fat lady sang her closing song.*

As a former pastor, my personal favorite would be the one about the rotund ladies in the church choir — but I digress. And the good news is — no matter which of the three is correct, she has yet to sing. It's not over!

The Return of Sam

My name is Samuel Anderson. *Pastor* "Sam" Anderson. *Doctor* Sam Anderson. I have more "degrees than a thermometer" and, in the words of a former church member, "have been educated beyond my intelligence." All true.

And yet, with all of that education it has been a little over a year since I was asked to leave First Church. My severance package is long gone, and I can't find a job!

No church in the area will seriously consider me since I am "damaged goods." Oh, I have had a few "nibbles" from various churches, but that is as far as it has gone; I never make it to the level of an interview. Apparently, any time one of the search committee members from an interested church contacts someone at First Church, they will hear some disparaging reason as to why I was asked to leave. I can't prove that, but it's what I believe.

I have even tried to find secular employment, but no one seems to be interested in hiring a washed-up preacher with only a few years left until retirement. The Lord certainly seems to have a way of closing doors!

Steve's Church

Rebecca and I have joined Steve Caldwell's church—Trinity Church. We have slowly taken on a few responsibilities. Rebecca keeps the nursery during evening worship services, and I teach a men's Bible class.

I admit I enjoy sitting with Rebecca in church. For years I was on one side of the pulpit and she was on the other. Now we are together!

One problem: men that are called to preach make terrible church members. I find myself listening to Steve preach and, while I enjoy his messages, I constantly think of better illustrations he could have used, or better points he could have made.

Rebecca notices my uneasiness. On the way home one Sunday, she asks, "Sam, what's wrong?"

"Nothing's wrong, Rebecca. Why do you ask?"

"Sam, it just seems like you are in another world every time we go to church. I see you flipping to other passages in your Bible while Steve is preaching; I see you writing during his sermons. But, quite frankly, you are *not* taking notes. You are writing sermons of your own!"

I reply, "I'm sorry, Rebecca. I will start listening to Steve. It's just…"

"It's just *what*, Sam?"

"I really miss preaching. I am like the prophet Jeremiah:

> *But if I say, "I will not remember Him or speak any more in His name," then in my heart it becomes like a burning fire shut up in my bones; and I am weary of holding it in, and I cannot endure it.*[4]

---

[4] Jeremiah 20:9.

That's exactly how I feel, Rebecca!"

"Sam, I am so sorry. Maybe Steve will let you fill in for him."

"He already *has*, Rebecca. And that just makes it worse! I am so frustrated! I don't know what to do. And, on top of all of that, you are the only one in our family with a job! I feel so useless."

"Sam, you stop that right now! I will not attend another one of your pity parties! You need to do something about your problems instead of sitting around trying to understand your circumstances."

"Yes dear."

"Samuel Anderson, you stop that 'yes dear' stuff right now! Turn the car around!"

"Why, Rebecca?"

"We are going back to talk to Steve. You are going to tell him exactly what is going on in your life, and then you are going to listen."

"But Rebecca, Steve has to rest before his message tonight. You remember how much I hated when people intruded upon my sacred nap time on Sunday afternoons."

"Sam, this is not open for debate. You turn this car around right now!"

"Yes dear."

Meeting with Steve

We arrive at Trinity Church, only to discover that Steve and his wife, Sarah, have left the building and have gone home for lunch. I try to reason with Rebecca: "Look, I agree that meeting with Steve is a good idea. Let me call and make an appointment."

"Oh, no you don't, Sam! I have lived with you for nearly forty years. You may be sincere *now*, but you will talk yourself out of it by tomorrow. We are going to Steve's house this very minute!" And then she gives me "the look."

"The look" reminds me of the joke about the husband being the head of the house, but the wife is the neck: she turns him wherever she wants him to go. So we go to Steve and Sarah's house.

I ring the doorbell; Steve answers. "Well hello, Sam and Rebecca. What a pleasant surprise! Come on in!" He turns to look toward the back of the house. "Sarah," he proclaims loudly, "we have guests!"

Sarah walks into the room, wiping her hands on a dishtowel. She smiles as she says, "Well, hello, Rebecca and Sam. How are you doing?"

"Oh, *I'm* fine, Sarah. It's *Sam* here," she says, as she points to me, "that needs some help."

"Well why don't you two come on in and have a seat. I am making lunch. I can just double the recipe."

I say, "Thanks, Sarah, but we don't want to be an intrusion."

"No trouble at all, Sam. You two talk to Steve; lunch will be ready in about thirty minutes."

"What's on your minds?" Steve asks. I look like the cat that swallowed the canary. I just sit there, glancing nervously around the room. My mouth is shut.

Rebecca speaks, "Steve, it's Sam—he is so miserable!"

Steve looks at me. "*Are* you miserable, Sam? Is something bothering you?"

I reply, "I really don't want to intrude upon your Sunday afternoon. I know you have to shift gears for your message tonight. Maybe we should talk about it some other time."

"No, Sam," Steve says. "I know Rebecca. If *she* thought it was important enough for us to talk about today, then we are going to talk about it today!"

I meekly reply, "Yes, *dears*," as I look first at Rebecca and then at Steve.

Rebecca says, "I think I will go help Sarah in the kitchen, and leave you two boys alone."

Rebecca exits the room. I feel abandoned, and a little threatened, as Steve asks the inevitable question, "What's wrong, Sam?"

"Steve, Rebecca has been right when she has been accusing me of having a pity party. I was doing great right after I was forced out of First Church, but it has been more than a year. And I don't even have a *job*!"

"I know, Sam. Sarah and I pray every morning for you and Rebecca—that the Lord will make His will clear to both of you."

"Thanks, Steve—I know you do. You have been a great pastor! It's just…"

"It's just *what*, Sam? I know. You miss preaching, don't you?"

"Steve, I didn't think that I would *ever* want to preach again. But I am like Jeremiah with the fire inside of my bones. And on some Sundays I think I am going to explode!"

"I can't imagine, Sam. Sarah and I will be gone for two weeks in June—would you like to preach for me while we are away?"

"I have thought about that, Steve. I really think that would just make things worse! To have another taste of preaching only to lose it again. I don't think I could handle it."

"I understand, Sam. I have a plan that I think will be exactly what you need." He looks at his day planner. "Sam, will you be going to the pastors' conference one month from tomorrow—on July 18th?"

"I don't know, Steve. I will have to check my calendar. Oh, wait—that day is clear! And any other day is clear, also! What's on your mind, Steve?"

"You'll see, Sam. I will pick you up at your house at 10:00 on the 18th. Okay?" I reply, "Okay."

We have lunch with Steve and Sarah. Sarah is one of the most gracious hostesses I have ever met. Steve is blessed! And, as I glance across the table at Rebecca, I think, "So am I."

The Pastors' Conference

July 18th. What is so significant about July 18th? Not knowing what Steve has planned is driving me crazy! I ask him, "What do you have in store for July 18th?

Steve says, "I have made some phone calls. We will attend the pastors' conference, and then go to lunch. After that, I have scheduled a meeting at 1:00."

I ask, "A meeting? What is the purpose of this meeting, Steve?"

And then he says the words that I absolutely cringe to hear. "You'll see."

I *hate* surprises. Several years ago, Rebecca planned a getaway for my birthday.

Amidst my objections, she hijacked me from my office at the church.

"I can't go Rebecca," I entreated. "I have work to do!"

"It's okay Sam," she said. "I have already cleared everything on your calendar for three days." For me, they were three *wretched* days!

I count the days as I wait for July 18th to roll around. As promised, Steve picks me up at 10:00. I ask, "What's going on, Steve?" Again he gives me the annoying refrain, "You'll see."

Steve and I walk into the pastors' conference. The other pastors seem genuinely happy to see me. The guest preacher preaches. We pray. And then, *finally*, we go to lunch. We large preachers certainly enjoy going to lunch!

One of the other pastors is unaware of my situation. "Where are you preaching now, Sam?"

Steve runs interference. "He's waiting for the Lord to open a door."

"Oh," the man replies. And then there is a deathly silence for the next few minutes.

Steve and I return to the associational office at 1:00. I look at the cars to see if I can discern the owners by the makes and years of their vehicles. I can't, but I do notice something: one of the cars is a rental. Could this be a clue?

At this point, I can identify with the description of Jesus in Isaiah 53:7:

> *He was oppressed and He was afflicted, yet He did not open His mouth; like a lamb that is led to slaughter, and like a sheep that is silent before its shearers, He did not open His mouth.*

I think, poetically, "Here comes *Sam*, the sacrificial *lamb*!"

Steve and I walk into the conference room. Five men are seated around the table; I recognize three of them: Ben Gilbert, the director of our denominational association, David Hanson from New Wine Church, and Mike Jackson from Faith Church.

Steve says, "Sam, you know Ben, David, and Mike." We reflexively shake each other's hands. "These other men are pastors from some large churches in other states. They have heard about the concepts David has incorporated at New Wine, and they are very interested in supporting a mission church following the New Wine model."

Ben jumps in, "And I am thrilled that David and the members at New Wine have applied for membership in our association of churches!"

I remark, "That's great, Ben. But why am *I* here?"

Ben continues, "Because the new church will need a pastor, and we believe you are just the man for the job!"

"Excuse me a moment," I say. "Steve, could I talk to you for a minute? Alone?" I rise. I motion for him to follow me as I walk toward the door. Steve and I leave the room and enter the hallway.

"Steve," I say, as I start to cry, "Why *me*? Why am *I* the man for the job? You can't possibly be serious!"

"But I *am* serious, Sam. And all of these other men agree with me. David has been talking to these two pastors for several months. They are now ready to proceed. I told them about your situation and they have prayed about it. *You* are our guy!"

I protest, "But they don't even know me, Steve!"

"No, Sam," Steve continues, "but they know *about* you. They know you have a heart for missions work. That, try though you might, you just haven't fit into a traditional church. They also know about your theological training, *Doctor* Anderson, and they are duly impressed!"

Silently, I turn and walk into the restroom. Ashamed by my tears, I wash and dry my reddened face. I rejoin Steve in the hallway. He asks, "Are you ready to go back in?"

I reply, "Yes, Steve."

We return to the meeting. "Sorry for the interruption, gentlemen," Steve says. "Now where were we?"

I recognize the first man to speak. I have heard him preach at several of our denomination conferences. His name is Carl Edwards, the pastor of a mega-church named "Unity." I think, "Unity Church? Wouldn't it be refreshing to serve in a church with a name and a reputation like that?"

Carl speaks. "Hello, Sam. My name is Carl. Carl Edwards. I have the privilege of serving as the senior pastor of a wonderful group of Christians at Unity Church. The people at Unity know that I have been talking with David about starting a church in this area, and they are all ready to get started. I have only one question for you: are *you* ready to get on board with us?"

I know what you are thinking. Now is the time to try to sound spiritual. I *should* say, "Let me pray about it." I don't. I excitedly exclaim, "Yes, sir, I am! I have been praying for months that God would open a door. This is a *portal!*"

"I agree, Sam," Carl says smilingly. And so does my brother over here. Sam, this is Lee Thompson." My mind races: "Lee Thompson—*the* Lee Thompson?" Carl tries to finish his introduction, "Sam, Lee is the pastor of…"

Without thinking, I blurt out, "I know who he is, Dr. Edwards. He's the pastor of Riverside Church. I have heard that Riverside is the fastest growing church in our denomination!"

Lee says, "I don't know about that, Sam. But I am pleased to meet you."

I shake his hand. I feel like a kid at a concert meeting a member of the band. I think, "Lee Thompson wants to help me start a church! This is beyond amazing—this is awesome!"

David steps into the conversation. "Steve and I have asked these two pastors, along with Ben and Mike, to meet with us here today. Sam, we want you to take some time to pray about this. If you choose to accept the offer to start the new church, Steve will become your coach. Ben and Mike will be your prayer and accountability partners. Will that be okay?"

I answer, "Sure, David—they are all wonderful men!"

He continues, "Sam, you will be placed on a one-year timeline. You will begin by going to Dr. Edwards' church to share your vision of the New Wine experiment. They have already pledged to pay your full salary and benefits for the first two years. When Dr. Thompson heard about the opportunity he said, 'We can do better than that!' And do you know what he meant?"

"David, I am afraid to ask," I reply.

Partners in Planting

"The people of Riverside Church have already purchased twenty acres of prime land on the highway, approximately one mile from your house. They will send a team of builders in a couple of months to begin the construction of your first building: an 'all-purpose' building. Basically, it will be a gym."

I am overwhelmed. Can this really be happening? I know! I am having a dream. No I'm not dreaming. I have died and gone to Heaven!

I fumble, "What can I say, Dr. Thompson? I don't know what to say."

Ben says, "I think you should say, 'Yes.'"

I can't help myself. I am a jokester, and a *fat* one at that. I say, "'Si,' 'oui,' and 'yes, *sir*!'"

"That's *great*, Sam," Lee says, emphatically. "And we would also like for you to speak at Riverside a week from Sunday. Will you be available?"

"Yes, sir, I will!"

"Tremendous! We would like to fly you and your wife to our town; we will put you up in our finest hotel and buy all of your meals. Sound good?"

"That sounds great, Dr. Thompson!"

Lee says, "Carl and I will need contact information from you, Sam."

Since I no longer carry business cards, I write my cell phone number and email address on two slips of paper. I hand a slip to each of them. Lee and Carl smile. They rise from the table. Carl speaks. "Sorry, gentlemen, but we have planes to catch. Please excuse us." We all shake hands. The two men climb into their shared rental car and drive off.

I look around the room at my remaining colleagues. I demand, "What just happened?"

Amused, Steve says, "I think you just found a job."

Mike takes things to a spiritual level. He says, "I feel like Moses in Exodus 3:6, "the place on which [I am] standing is holy ground!'"

We all nod in agreement. I ask, "What happens next?"

David looks around the table. He says, "I think we *all* know. Now is when the real work begins."

The Interlude

"Guess what, Rebecca" I say, as I stroll casually through the front door.

"What, Sam? Did you and Steve have a good time at the pastors' conference?"

"You could say that. In fact, you could say that we had a *great* time!"

"What happened?" she asks.

Partners in Planting

Unable to conceal my excitement, I shout, "I have a *job*! I am going to preach again! And I will finally have the opportunity to start a *new* church instead of going to another *traditional* one!"

"That *is* great news, Sam! Tell me all about it."

"Rebecca, I know you don't keep up with the churches in our denomination. But pastors from two of the largest churches were at the meeting today!"

"Why were *they* there, Sam?"

"One of the pastors, Carl Edwards, told me that his church wants to pay my salary and all of our expenses for *two years*!"

"*Two* years, Sam? I can't believe it!"

"That's only half of the news, Rebecca! The other pastor, Lee Thompson said that his church has already purchased twenty acres on the main highway only one mile from our house, and they are about to start the construction of our new building!"

Rebecca raises her hand and places it, palm out, on her forehead. She pretends to faint. "Water; I need water, Sam!" I run to the kitchen and come back with a glass of water. She says, "I was only kidding!" *I* drink the water.

I say, "It begins with an all-expense-paid trip to Lee Thompson's church a week from Sunday. They will fly us to their town and treat us royally." I jokingly say, "Do you think you might be able to go?"

Rebecca punches me, playfully, in the arm. "Ouch!" I say. "Where did you learn to hit like that?" She reminds me that she has two brothers.

She grins as she says, "You're a big baby, Samuel Anderson!" And then she begins to frantically rehearse, "What should I wear? Who will take care of feeding our pets? When is our flight?"

I place both hands on her shoulders. "Relax, Rebecca. Dr. Thompson and his people will make all the arrangements. We just have to get on the plane."

Riverside Church

Dr. Thompson's secretary calls me on my cell phone, and I answer. She says, "Hello, Sam. This is Amy McGregor. I am Dr. Thompsons's personal assistant." I think, "Personal assistant? Impressive!" She continues, "I understand that you will be the speaker for our morning church services one week from Sunday. Could you and your wife fly out next Thursday afternoon?"

I respond, "My wife, Rebecca, works until around 4:00. The earliest we could arrive at the airport would be 6:00."

Partners in Planting

We share a brief moment of silence. I hear the faint clicking of the keys on Amy's keyboard. She says, "I have the Delta™ website on my computer screen. They have a flight leaving your town at 7:30 and arriving here at 9:30. Will that give the two of you enough time?" I reply, "Yes, Amy, it will."

"Sam," she says, "I just need your full name and your wife's so that I can book your flights."

I respond, "My name is 'Samuel Elijah Anderson.' My wife's name is 'Rebecca Ruth Anderson.'"

After another brief moment, she informs me, "I've got it. I will send your e-tickets to you as an email attachment to the address you provided for Dr. Thompson. We are all looking forward to meeting you and Rebecca next Sunday."

Obligingly, I say, "Thank you, Amy."

Our flight is uneventful, other than the fact that Rebecca and I are sitting in *first class seats*! She and I discover that the flight attendants are much more attentive at this level. They ask such questions as, "Would you like anything else, Mr. Anderson? And for you, Mrs. Anderson?"

We eat on *real* plates with *real* silverware. And they serve us *real* desserts: pecan pie! A chubby guy (like *me*) could get used to this!

One of the couples from Riverside picks us up at the airport. They introduce themselves as Jeff and Susanna Whiteside. Jeff tells us, "We are delighted to have you visiting with us this weekend!"

I thank him and ask, "How many people should we expect in your services on a typical Sunday morning?"

Jeff replies—"Susanna and I typically go to the early service—about 2,600 in that meeting, I *think*. We probably have around 3,000 in the late service."

I quickly do the math. I will be speaking to a total of almost 6,000 people on Sunday! I give Rebecca a look of subdued excitement. She just stares back, wide-eyed, at me.

We arrive at the hotel—if you can call it that! It looks like a New York skyscraper! We check in and are escorted—that's right, *escorted* to our rooms by a uniformed bellhop, complete with the gray cap with black trim. I offer to give him a $20.00 tip, but he refuses. He says, "I am *also* a member at Riverside Church. We are glad you are here!" He hands the room keys to me, and then quietly leaves.

Rebecca and I survey our suite. The spacious rooms make our home look tiny! "Well, dear," I say, "welcome to the Big League!"

She responds, "Big League, nothing. This is Heaven!" I smile as I think, "Rebecca deserves this royal treatment, *especially* when someone else is picking up the tab! As you well know, my favorite word is 'free.' Spell it with me: 'F R E E ! '"

We go to the restaurant, located in a room adjacent to the lobby. We both stare at the prices on the menu. We finally order meals that would cost the equivalent of two weeks' groceries back home. After glancing carefully over both of my shoulders, I whisper to Rebecca, "This is living!" Guiltily, she agrees.

We finish our meals. The waiter asks the humorous question, "And did we save room for dessert?" I speak for both of us, "Yes, we did!" And, like the rest of the food, the desserts are *fabulous*! We extend our compliments to the chef as I sign the check that will add the cost of the meals to our room charges. We return to our room.

In a matter of moments, my cell phone starts to ring. "Hello," I say.

The voice on the other end asks, "Sam?"

I reply, "Yes, it is."

He says, "Sam, this is Lee Thompson. Are you and Rebecca enjoying your accommodations?"

"Yes, sir we are! And everything is amazing!"

"I'm glad you and Rebecca are enjoying yourselves, Sam. As you know, you have a couple of days before you speak to our folks. I would like to meet briefly with the two of you tomorrow morning—say around 10:00—for a late breakfast there in the hotel. Will that work for you?"

"It certainly will. We will see you in the morning."

Rebecca and I sleep well in what must have been the biggest bed either of us has ever seen. Our king-sized bed at home, like our house, is dwarfed by our current surroundings. We sleep in until 8:00, pray, get dressed, and go down to the lobby.

Dr. Thompson has already arrived. He is dressed in an expensive suit and reading the newspaper. I clear my throat. He glances up immediately and smiles. He places the newspaper on the table and motions for us to sit.

I say, "Dr. Thompson, this is my wife, Rebecca."

He interrupts. "Lee. Just call me Lee." He looks at me as he says, "Unless, of course, you want me to address *you* as *Doctor* Anderson?"

I reply, "That won't be necessary, *Lee*. And this is my wife, *Doctor* Rebecca Anderson."

Lee turns to face her. "So you are a doctor, also."

She replies, "No, Sam is just having a little fun."

I rise to her defense. "But she does have two masters' degrees!" Lee smiles appreciatively as he says, "It's nice to meet you, Rebecca. We are so happy to have the two of you here with us. How about some breakfast," he says as he nods toward the dining room. For my benefit, he says, "It's a *buffet*, Sam!"

I think, "I can handle that!" I say, "That's tremendous. I am like Paul: I believe in *buffet*ing my body."

Rebecca gives me "the look." "Sam, I think Paul said *buffeting*—as in striking it; beating it up!"

"You believe what you want, Rebecca. I will believe what I want."

Dr. Thompson raises his hands in an attempt to referee our disagreement. He says, "The winner of this theological debate is..." he pauses for effect. He finishes, "*Rebecca*. But *I* am with *you*, Sam. Let's eat!" I fill up two plates, with sideboards, as Rebecca carefully places a few morsels of fruit on hers.

We speak very little until we have finished our meals. Lee then asks, "Did you two sleep well?" I reply, "We sure did. Thank you, again, for taking such good care of us."

He waves off my compliment. He says, "Sam, the Bible says in Matthew 10:10, 'the worker is worthy of his support.' You and Rebecca have been two of God's choicest servants for years. We at Riverside are more than happy to have this opportunity to serve *you*!"

Rebecca responds, "Sam and I really do appreciate this. At times it has seemed that the Lord had forgotten us."

Lee assures her, "No, He hasn't, Rebecca. And I believe He is about to prove His love for the two of you in a big way!" He looks at me as he says, "Sam, as I mentioned, I am only going to be with you briefly this morning. You know: the curse of the *big* church."

I nod as I say, "I understand, Lee."

He continues, "I just wanted to touch base with you about this Sunday morning's services. We will have two: 9:30 and 11:00. You will be the guest speaker for both. You will have 25 minutes to speak—no more and, (he smiles) unless you want to replace me as the pastor, no less. You know the adage, 'No one has ever complained that the message was too *short*!'" We all share a hearty laugh.

Lee resumes, "As a little background, Sam, David Hanson spoke to our people two months ago. That's when we decided to buy the land and build the building there in your town. We didn't know about *you* at the time. We have left the selection of the new pastor for the church start to David's discretion. We have totally endorsed his choice to call you as the new pastor."

I give him an "aw shucks" look. "That's great, Lee! I am really looking forward to speaking at Riverside on Sunday, and to our

Partners in Planting

ongoing partnership in the future." Rebecca just nods.

Lee stands up. He says, "Sam, that's all I have." He places a booklet into my hand. He resumes, "Here is a church bulletin for Sunday morning, and a valet ticket to pick up your rental car in the hotel garage. Have a great time, enjoy the next couple of days sight-seeing or shopping, and we will see you on Sunday. Here's my private cell phone number if either of you should need anything before Sunday."

"We will let you know if we do," I reply. "And thanks again!'

He smiles. "You're welcome, Sam and Rebecca. We will see you on Sunday!"

Rebecca and I take a guided tour of the city. What a big place! Rebecca is a cosmopolitan girl—she has missed all of the hustle and bustle. I haven't!

I am reminded of a popular television sitcom that aired in 1966, appropriately named "Green Acres®." Rebecca and I apparently have the "Green Acres® Syndrome." We are mirror images of Oliver and Lisa Douglas, the husband and wife characters on the show. Other than that, we are *fully* compatible in *every* way.

Saturday night arrives. Rebecca and I have truly enjoyed our time together. It is now time to write the infamous, "Saturday Night Special." No, not the *pistol*. The *sermon*! I turn on my laptop. I conduct a word search through all of my old sermons in an effort to find one that will impress the people of Riverside Church. I finally realize that none of my sermons will ever begin to compare to one of Lee Thompson's!

I decide to do the safe thing: I will read a passage from the Bible and tell my story. I could read the passage from Matthew 9 about the new wine and the old wineskins, but I'm guessing that David has already done that.

Since Rebecca and I are moving up in years, I decide to read one of my favorite passages: Joshua 14:6-12. Rebecca and I try to sleep, but we are both excited about the opportunity the Lord has given to us.

Sunday morning arrives! We drive our rental car to Riverside Church. We park in one of the *guest* spots near the building. We are promptly met by a man wearing both a conspicuous name badge and a broad smile. He says, "Hello, folks." He motions with his thumb toward his badge as he says, "My name is 'John.' We are so glad to have you visiting with us this morning! Have you worshiped with us before?"

I answer, "No, John, we haven't."

John says, "Then please come with me. We have something special for the two of you!" As we walk across the parking lot with John, he deftly, but unobtrusively, asks questions to discover such information as our names, where we are from, and why we are here.

Partners in Planting

John leads us into one of the massive buildings, down a wide hallway, and into a spacious room. The sign above the door tells us we are entering the "Welcome Center." As a rotund preacher, the first thing *I* notice is the table literally overflowing with doughnuts and muffins—the traditional ingredients of a continental breakfast. But then, following my keen sense of smell, I perceive several large platters filled with scrambled eggs and sausage!

John, apparently understanding the dangers of obstructing my path to the feast, says, "I will let you help yourselves." He gingerly takes two steps back and waits for us to fill our plates. He directs us to a small table in the corner of the room. He walks over to an information table and speaks to a young lady.

After we are seated and have begun to eat, John returns to our table. He is accompanied by the young lady. She is also wearing a name badge. John introduces her to us, anyway, as "*Karen.*" Turning his attention to her, he says, "Karen, these are my two new friends, Sam and Rebecca. Sam will be our special speaker in both services this morning!"

John rises to leave as Karen picks up the conversation. "Sam and Rebecca, we are delighted to have you visiting with us this morning! And, Sam, we are *especially* pleased that you will be sharing in our morning services. You must be the couple we have heard so much about. You are starting a new church we, at Riverside, are helping to sponsor. Is that right?"

"Yes it is Karen," I say, as I finish a bite of eggs and carefully wipe the corners of my mouth. I think, "Someone must have informed the Welcome Center staff that Rebecca and I were coming. They were *obviously* on the lookout for us. This is quite impressive!"

"Well, Sam," she says, "I can't wait to hear your message. You two enjoy your meals. I will be stationed at the desk over there (she points). Just come over when you are ready, and I will take you to our sanctuary."

Rebecca speaks for the first time, "Thank you, Karen."

"You're welcome, Rebecca." And then Karen returns to her spot behind the desk.

"Wow, Rebecca. I wish our visitors at First Church would have received *this* kind of treatment!"

"Just eat Sam," she replies.

We finish our meals. Two friendly teenagers walk up to pick up our plates and silverware. One smilingly says, "I hope you enjoyed your meals."

I say, "Thank you, we did. Very much!"

We walk over to the desk. We wait while Karen finishes a conversation with some of the other first time guests. She turns her attention to us: "Sam and Rebecca! Are you ready to go?" We nod.

Partners in Planting

Karen leads us down a massive hallway. The ceilings must be at least 40 feet tall! She says, "Would you like to stop at the restroom before we go into the sanctuary?"

Rebecca and I look at each other. No words are needed after nearly forty years of marriage. She says, "No, Karen, we're fine."

"Then let's go in," she says, as she greets the man that is holding the door open for us. "This is our sanctuary!" She sweeps her hand around, pointing to various places in the room like Vanna White points to the letters on the game show, *Wheel of Fortune*.®

Lee Thompson spots us immediately. He motions for us to join him on the platform. Rebecca gives me "the look" to let me know she isn't comfortable standing in front of hundreds of people. I take her hand—the one I asked her father for in marriage—and we mount the steps on the way to the mountaintop.

"Good morning, you two!" he exclaims. "Have a seat in those two chairs right over there." We sit.

The pre-service music, performed by a full orchestra, begins to play. Lee makes small talk with Rebecca and me as the choir begins to assemble.

I turn to Rebecca. I whisper loudly, "There must be at least 200 people in that choir."

Lee, eavesdropping on our exchange, says, "It's more like 350!" I gulp!

The announcements are made. The offering is *taken* — or, rather, *received*. Lee rises to introduce us. "Stand up, Sam and Rebecca," he says. Dutifully, we stand up.

He reminds the congregation, "David Hanson was our guest speaker several months ago. He told us about the exciting way God is using him in building the New Wine Church. He challenged us to start another church in his area using the concepts he has developed in his church. And, I am excited to say, we have *unanimously* agreed!"

Lee places his arms around the two of us and says, "And this is the couple for which we have been praying. They will lead this new church. Let's see if I can remember which one is which?" He laughs as he looks in my direction and pulls me closer. "This is Sam Anderson." He turns to face Rebecca. "And this is his wife, Rebecca. We are so thrilled the two of you have come to share with us today!" He releases us. We return to our seats. "Sam will speak immediately after our special music."

A young lady moves to the front of the platform as the orchestra begins to play. I don't hear a word of the song as I scan the room. This is definitely the largest group I have ever addressed! She finishes and I stand.

I begin, "Rebecca and I have been overwhelmed at the kindnesses you have shown to us for the last few days. Your pastor is a wonderful man, and we have both grown to love him," I say, as I glance back to the place where Lee is seated. He smiles, first at me, and then at the members of the congregation.

"I would like to invite you to open your Bibles this morning to the book of Joshua, chapter fourteen, verses six through twelve. I will be reading from the New American Standard Version:

> *Then the sons of Judah drew near to Joshua in Gilgal, and Caleb the son of Jephunneh the Kenizzite said to him, "You know the word which the Lord spoke to Moses the man of God concerning you and me in Kadesh-barnea. I was forty years old when Moses the servant of the Lord sent me from Kadesh-barnea to spy out the land, and I brought word back to him as it was in my heart. Nevertheless my brethren who went up with me made the heart of the people melt with fear; but I followed the Lord my God fully. So Moses swore on that day, saying, 'Surely the land on which your foot has trodden will be an inheritance to you and to your children forever, because you have followed the Lord my God fully.' Now behold, the Lord has let me live, just as He spoke, these forty-five years, from the time that the Lord spoke this word to Moses, when Israel walked in the wilderness; and now behold, I am eighty-five years old today. I am still as*

strong today as I was in the day Moses sent me; as my strength was then, so my strength is now, for war and for going out and coming in. Now then, give me this hill country about which the Lord spoke on that day, for you heard on that day that Anakim were there, with great fortified cities; perhaps the Lord will be with me, and I will drive them out as the Lord has spoken."

I am tempted to tell the people that Rebecca is a few months older than I, but the Holy Spirit restrains me from making a joke at her expense. Besides, she is already uncomfortable enough sitting in front of this large audience. I continue.

"The Lord called me to preach when I was 26 years old. Rebecca and two of our children moved with me so that I could attend the seminary. And, lo and behold, a few months before I graduated, child number three mysteriously appeared!" The people laugh—a good sign!

"We began a long journey together of nearly thirty years of ministry. We walked through the wilderness of serving five churches, all filled with *wonderful* people, but never really connecting with them in a truly meaningful way. I was always thinking, 'Is there something wrong with *them*—or is it with *me*?' I could never seem to get a handle on it."

Partners in Planting

"Rebecca and I overstayed the customary three years' welcome at our last church. Needless to say, we 'went through the fire!' But do you know what? Hebrews 12:29 tells us that 'our *God* is a consuming fire!'"

Lee shouts, "Amen!" A bevy of church members follow suit. I think, "Here we go!"

"And not only that! When the three Hebrew boys were cast into the fire, *somebody* was standing right there along with them. Who was it?"

The church members respond, "Jesus!"

I affirm, "That's right, it was *Jesus*! He *is* the fire, and He stands with us *in* the fire!"

One man stands up in the middle of the room. He points at me as he says, "Tell it, preacher!" I begin to smile.

Following his counsel, I *tell it*. "Having gone through God's purifying fire I have now, for the first time in my life, fully experienced and begun to understand the amazing mercy of our Lord Jesus Christ!"

Several people echo the word, "Mercy," followed by a few more shouting, "Amen!"

I resume. "A friend of mine in the seminary named Ken Stevens once told the members of his Sunday school class, 'Marriage is like a bank—it pays dividends when you show interest.'" Lee chuckles.

-"Mercy is also like a bank. When you invest a little of it in the lives of other people,

God places it all back into your life—with *interest*! You have all discovered that, when you give financially to the Lord, He always gives you more so that you can give it back to Him again." Lee shouts, "Amen," followed by a *tiny* chorus of others. I think, "Money seems to be a touchy subject in *every* church."

I point, sweepingly, to the crowd. "And so it is with mercy. Rebecca will be the first one to tell you that I am not perfect." I look at her. She nods vigorously in agreement. "In fact, I am far from it! As Paul was 'chief of sinners',[5] I have been the chief of the unmerciful Christians. I grew up without mercy from my earthly father. I have been a husband without any mercy for my wonderful wife. I have raised three children apart from mercy. And I have ministered, without mercy, to the members of five churches." I start to cry. Lee steps up and places a strong hand upon my shoulder. Now the tears really begin to flow!

A minute later I regain my composure. I glance back and say, "Thank you, Lee." He smiles paternally and returns to his seat.

I continue: "Having seen a room void of mercy—a vacuum of mercy, if you will—in a church business meeting, I now have a vivid understanding of this wonderful blessing that

---

[5] 1 Timothy 1:15, King James Version.

can come only from God! By the grace of God, I have discontinued my 'pity parties,' and have begun ministering to others that have also been hurt by the statements that were made in the same meeting. And do you know what? The more I have *given* mercy in ministry to others, the more mercy I have *received* from the Lord."

"Dwight L. Moody was a powerful evangelist from yesteryear. Some ladies were praying that he would have a fresh encounter with the Lord. Their prayers were answered one day as Moody was walking down the street. He rushed into a friend's house and asked to borrow an upstairs room. The friend showed him to the room. Moody ran inside and fell on his knees. He later said of the incident:"[6]

> *One day in New York — what a day! I can't describe it! I seldom refer to it! It is almost too sacred to name! I can only say God revealed Himself to me! I had such an experience of love that I had to ask Him to stay His hand! I went to preaching again. The sermons were no different. I did not present any new truth. Yet hundreds were converted. I would not be back where I was before that blessed experience.*

---

[6] Tan, Paul Lee, *Encyclopedia of 7,700 Illustrations*, (Garland, Texas: Bible Communications, Inc.) 1996.

"And so it has been with *my* experience of mercy! Having God's abundance of mercy in my life has been worth all of the attacks, all of the pain, and all of the fire that He has safely carried Rebecca and me through!" The people are now chanting, "Amen! Hallelujah! Praise His name!"

"I have experienced this mercy primarily because I have been a 'square peg in a round hole' — the wrong *preacher* in the wrong *church* at the wrong *time*. God has now, through the generous support and mercy from folks like you here at Riverside Church, opened a door of ministry that I would never have anticipated! You have revived my spirit! Because of your encouragement I, like Caleb in the book of Joshua, have a renewed desire to take on the giants! You have refreshed my vision for conquering that mountain! I feel young again!" Once again, the tears start to flow. Lee points inconspicuously at me as he nods toward Rebecca. In response, she rises and places her arms around me. The entire congregation stands to its feet. They applaud for a full minute before the ovation finally ends.

Lee steps forward as Rebecca and I step back. He gives the invitation. The altar is filled with people praying for us and for the new work. Eleven people accept Jesus Christ as their Lord and Savior, and eight families join the church.

Partners in Planting

Lee says to Rebecca and me, "Come into my office and rest. You still have one more sermon to preach!"

We retreat to Lee's office. He leaves us alone. Rebecca says, "Wow, Sam! Did you mean all that?"

"Of course I did!"

"Then I am with you—one hundred percent!"

"Rebecca," I say, "this has been one of the happiest days of my life. The way things have been going in our lives I was beginning to think that I might lose you!"

"Sam," she says tenderly, but firmly, "you will *never* lose me. I am your biggest fan!" We embrace.

Suddenly, we hear the doorknob turn. We quickly separate and act nonchalant, just in time to see Lee and five other people walking through the doorway. He smiles and says, "Did we come at a bad time?"

Rebecca, blushing, says, "No, Lee, you folks come right on in."

"Okay, Rebecca," Lee tells her, "If you say so."

Lee introduces the five people to us. I am certain that neither Rebecca nor I will be able to remember their names. "Rebecca and Sam, these five men and women are the team members that have been assigned to making the land purchase and supervising the building project for the church you two will be establishing back home. They will be working with you in the design of the initial building and the layout for your future auditorium and educational space."

I respond, "We are glad to meet you!"

We spend the next thirty minutes discussing everything from the New Wine Church planting principles to future church growth and expansion. The five team members leave; Lee prays with us.

Much to Rebecca's chagrin, I stop to tell Lee a joke just before we return to the auditorium:

> *A young man sang a solo at the local church. When he finished the people all shouted, "Sing it again!" So he sang it again. They chimed, "Sing it again!" So he sang it the third time. They cried "Sing it again!"*
>
> *The young man held up his right hand and said, "Thank you, but three times is my limit."*
>
> *A man rose in the back of the room. He looked at the soloist and said, "No, you will sing it until you get it right!"*

"Lee," I said, "I am going to *preach* it until I get it right!" He gives me a courtesy laugh. Rebecca gives me "the look," as if to say, "You had to do it, didn't you?" I return her look as I verbally answer her thoughts, "Yes, I did!"

Partners in Planting

I preach it again, and I cry—again, but at totally different times during the message. The response during the invitation is, once again, breathtaking.

Rebecca and I say our goodbyes to the fine people of Riverside Church. We return to the hotel and collect our belongings. We make the return flight back home, once again enjoying the amenities of first-class seating. The next morning I call Steve and David to give them a report of our trip.

David says, "Remember what I told you: *now* is when the work *really* begins!"

I respond, "I remember." And then I start to wonder, "What exactly does he mean by that?"

My question was destined to receive a speedy response!

A New Beginning for a Church

Several years ago, I read a "Wizard of Id"[7] comic strip. It consisted of three frames. The first frame showed the king standing on the balcony addressing the peasants. In the second frame, he stated, "This kingdom is run by trial and error." The third frame showed one of the peasants talking to another peasant. He said, "When is the *trial*?"

The modern church, like the king's management of the kingdom, has made many errors. It has veered off the path of the New Testament concept of "church." It is traveling, full-speed, in the wrong direction! And, unless we return to God's pattern, we are due for the beginning of a real trial!

---

[7] Dogs of C-Kennel, © 2010 Mick Mastroianni, all rights reserved.

Is there hope? Can the church possibly return to its Biblical moorings? The answer is a resounding "Yes," as long as the Lord is involved. "God plus one man is *still* a majority!"

David Hanson, Steve Caldwell, and I meet together. I am still "on cloud nine" from my trip with Rebecca to Riverside Church.

"David," I begin, "I have both a statement and a question."

David replies, "Okay Sam, go ahead."

"First, the statement: I am glad that you are leading your church to join our denomination. I would be the first to admit our group has its problems. But, as far as I know, our overall theology is still the closest to being in agreement with the Bible."

He says, "I agree, Sam. What is your question?"

"My question is, 'Why did you pick *me* to serve as the pastor of the new church start?'"

Steve interrupts. "David, may I answer this one?"

David nods. "Sure Steve, go ahead."

Steve winks as he says, "Sam we picked you because we felt sorry for you." David hits Steve in the arm. "Ouch," Steve says. "Have you considered a career in boxing?"

David looks at me. "We picked *you*, Sam, because you love Jesus, you don't seem to fit into a traditional church, and you are *available* to start immediately."

"All true, David," I concur. "So we have a building and I have two years' salary and benefits. I am ready to start next Sunday!"

"Slow down, Sam" David says. "We are entering a process that will take nearly a year to complete. We have already set the target date for the grand opening of the new church for one year after you select your ministry team."

I ask, "Ministry *team*?"

David continues, "All in due time Sam, all in due time." David hands two copies of some sort of handbook to me. The cover says "New Wine Training Manual." He explains that he and several others have recently compiled the book. He says, "Sam, here is a little 'light reading' for you and your primary ministry partner, Rebecca, as the two of you begin your journey with New Wine Church. I would imagine it will take you at least a week to read through it. Call me when you're finished, and we will begin the training process."

I am puzzled. I ask, "Training process?" He says, "Just read it, and then call me, Sam."

I concur, "Okay, David, I will."

As if he has an afterthought, David mentions, "And here is a copy of one of the papers I wrote as I was working on my doctorate in the seminary: 'A Composite Model of Church Leadership.'"[8]

---

[8] See Appendix A.

Playfully, I ask, "I didn't know that. Should I call you *Doctor* Hanson?" I notice that he is mildly irritated.

He responds, "No. *David* will do just fine."

Training Barnabas and Saul

I take the two copies of the manual home with me. I hand one copy to Rebecca. Since she is the only member of our household currently with a job, I have a fairly good idea how she is going to react. Without letting me down, she protests, "When am I going to have time to read this massive tome?"

I timidly reply, "Do you remember how you used to read my textbooks for me in college?" She nods. I continue, "And you would highlight the main ideas?" She nods again, but by this time she is glaring at me. I continue, "I will do that for you." And then she gives me a look that speaks much more loudly than any words. I reply. "No, *really*, I will." Rebecca's irritated expression never changes.

I walk into the living room, and sit down in my favorite chair. I begin to read David's seminary paper, entitled, "A Composite Model of Church Leadership."[9] I think, "This guy is pretty smart!" Apparently he was beginning to entertain thoughts about starting a church a long time ago: the date on the title page is May 13, 1999! And then it occurs to me: "David must be older than I *thought*."

I scan through my copy of the handbook. "David thinks I should be able to read all of this in one week? He must be kidding!" I take out a Highlighter™ and begin to read. Two weeks later, I finish. I give my highlighted copy to Rebecca, take her copy, and call David. I tell him, "I'm ready, David. I have finished reading the training manual."

He says, "That's great, Sam. Why don't you come by the office on Monday morning around 8:00?"

I agree. "Okay, David."

I arrive a little early — 7:45. I have learned this trick from a former boss. He insisted that, if I was going to work for him, I would be wise to err on the early side than to take the risk of coming in late. Old habits certainly do die hard.

David's secretary recognizes me. She says, as she points to David's office door, "Go on in, Sam. David will be here in a few minutes."

"Thank you," I respond. I walk in. I have visited David's office once before, but I have never had the opportunity to look around.

---

[9] See Appendix A.

"Interesting place," I think to myself. David has his office decorated in four segments: degrees and accomplishments on one wall, pictures of his family on another, artifacts and pictures from mission trips he has taken on a third.

But the most fascinating wall in his office is dedicated to the Word of God. A picture of a giant eagle with an inscription taken from Isaiah 40:31 is the centerpiece:

> *Yet those who wait for the Lord will gain new strength; they will mount up with wings like eagles, they will run and not get tired, they will walk and not become weary.*

I catch myself whispering the word, "Amen!" Another verse has a picture of a beautiful sunrise with the caption: "that I may know Him and the power of His resurrection and the fellowship of His sufferings, being conformed to His death."[10]

David walks in. "Hello, Sam," he says. "Are you admiring my office?"

I flash back to the days when I had a bigger office than David's. *His* office is bigger now. In fact, *any* office is bigger than mine. I don't have one. I smile jealously as I say, "Yes I was, David. I especially like the Bible verses!"

---

[10] Philippians 3:10.

Partners in Planting

David resumes, "Thanks, Sam. I have learned over the years the immeasurable value of praying God's Word back to Him. Every morning the first item on my agenda is to look at this focal wall and pray. Want to join me?" I nod and say, "Sure David."

David walks over to join me at the wall. He begins his prayer with Isaiah 40:31. "Dear Lord, I thank you for the majesty of the eagle—the way he transcends the obstacles of this world. I thank you that when I wait upon you that you give me the strength I need to carry on. I know that you want me to be busy serving You while I wait. But I also know that nothing of eternal significance will take place until You show up on the scene. Even so, as Your Word says in Revelation 22:20, 'maranatha'—come, Lord Jesus! Would you like to give it a try, Sam?"

I respond, "Okay." And then I plunge right in. "Father, I thank You that You have made Yourself known to us through Your Son, Jesus Christ. I want to experience You today, and to know You better. I thank You that the same power You demonstrated when Jesus rose from the dead is available today—to *us*! I thank You for allowing Your people to suffer, because sharing in the sufferings of Christ helps us to become more like Him. And, Lord, I look forward to the day when this life will end and I will spend eternity with You!"

David is pleased. He congratulates me. "That's good, Sam. Are you ready to get started?" I nod. "Okay—you and I will work together this morning. Steve will work with you this afternoon." And then he says jokingly, "And, if you are a good disciple, we will give you the night off." I smile. He continues, "The first thing we want to do is to define our relationship. You have my permission to think of me as wearing many hats—your mentor, your coach, your cheerleader. But I am *not* your boss and you do *not* work for me. I am here for *you*. I want to be *your* assistant as you start your new church."

I ask him, "David, what did you mean when you said, 'the night off?' Are we meeting again tomorrow? He nods affirmatively. I protest, "I thought Steve said you and I would only meet monthly?"

David resumes, "Sam, I guess you are referring to the time when Steve told you that the two you would meet once a week to discuss your observations about New Wine?" I nod. He continues, "He also said that the three of us would meet once a month to examine my game plan for transforming churches, and we would all meet with Bob Moritz to plan your reentry into the ministry?"[11]

"That's right, David."

"The plans have changed, Sam. You and I will meet four mornings a week—Monday through Thursday—with Fridays off for good behavior!"

I say, sarcastically, "Thank you, David."

"You're welcome, Sam. You told me on the phone that you had finished reading through the manual. What did you think about it?"

"It's amazing, David! You have done a tremendous amount of work in putting it together!"

David responds, "Not really. It took some work to compile it, but the manual is really the result of years of trial and error. One thing we have learned about the ways of the Lord during the formation of New Wine Church is that He would rather have us do the wrong things for the right reason than the right things for the wrong reason."

"Say that again, David. Are you telling me God wants us to do the *wrong* things?"

"No, Sam. I am saying He is more concerned with our attitudes than He is with our actions. He is more blessed by our 'whys' than He is by our 'whats'."

---

[11] Scott Moore, <u>Mercy! God's Vindication of Pastors and Other Workers Terminated from Christian Ministry</u>.

"I am with you David. So did you make some mistakes along the way?"

"More than you could count! But we have learned from them and, I believe, we have arrived—rather, we have progressed—to the place where we, as a church, have an uncanny resemblance to the New Testament Church." I smile in affirmation. "And our 'mistakes,' as you call them, have really been blessings in disguise. And, on many occasions, the Holy Spirit stopped us before we made some really big ones (Acts 16:6)! By the grace of God, our prayer is that you will avoid our mistakes altogether!"

"Amen to that David."

"Sam, the first month we will spend together will be strictly educational. You will learn how the manual applies to the process of starting a new church. We will cover a lot of ground, and I hope you will ask plenty of questions."

"I will, David. In fact, I have one right now. When do we eat?"

"Spoken like a preacher, Sam. Spoken like a preacher. We will have lunch with Steve at noon, after which I will leave in order to take care of some church business. Steve will take over with you for the afternoon session."

"Thanks, David. I am glad we cleared that up."

"Sam, this morning, *before* we go to lunch, I want us to look together at the seminary paper.[12] The thoughts we have gleaned from that paper have saved us from making many monumental mistakes as we were forming New Wine Church."

The Seminary Paper

David asks, "As we begin, what did *you* think about the paper, Sam?"

"I thought it was very impressive, David! I used to work on an assembly line during my college days—everything from welding to winding electric motors."

"Well, Sam," David replies, "you must be a jack of all trades."

I complete his thought, "And master of none!"

"I doubt that, Sam. And when you and I have finished working together you will be a master of planting churches. Let's get back to the seminary paper. As I mentioned, this information stopped us from making a serious error in the early days of New Wine Church. Let me show you why. Turn to page three in your

---

[12] See Appendix A.

Training Manual. You will notice the following diagram:"

I turn to page three. "Okay, David. Explain it to me."

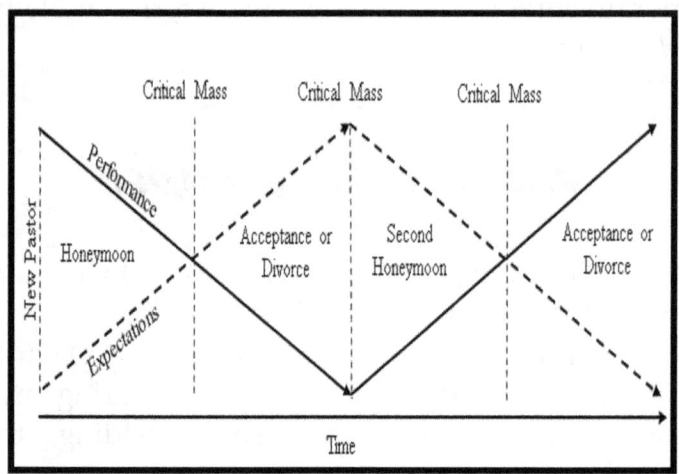

"Unfortunately, Sam, this chart describes too many of the churches in our denomination. It is a picture of the 'Saul Church.' And I am *certain* it describes the church from which you have recently resigned: First Church!"

I am fascinated. He continues, "When you arrived at First Church several years ago, your performance level was at its peak. You naturally wanted to please the Lord, but you also aspired to make a good impression on your new church members."

"So far so good, David."

"And on *their* part, the church members' expectations of you were extremely low. They were simply glad to have a new pastor on board. Conversely, *your* expectations for the church members were extremely low and they were on *their* best behavior."

"Okay, David. I can see that."

"But Sam, over time, things began to degenerate. Performance on both sides began to drop as expectations on both sides began to rise. They intersected at a point I call 'critical mass.' And it was about that time that the lynching party got the noose and hung you out to dry."

"That's incredible David! How did you know that?"

"It happened to me, too. You aren't the only pastor that has been asked to resign or has been terminated by a church."

"I know David. And I remember that you left our denomination and started New Wine as a result."

"That's right, Sam. And I had a lot of time to pray about my situation and understand why it happened."

"Okay, David. What could have been done differently?"

"Thanks for making it easy for me, David. You're like the fish that jumped right into the boat—no reeling necessary." I smile. "So my natural response to being terminated was to react. I thought, 'If I am going to start a church, it certainly won't be anything like the one I left!'

That's when I came up with the next diagram":

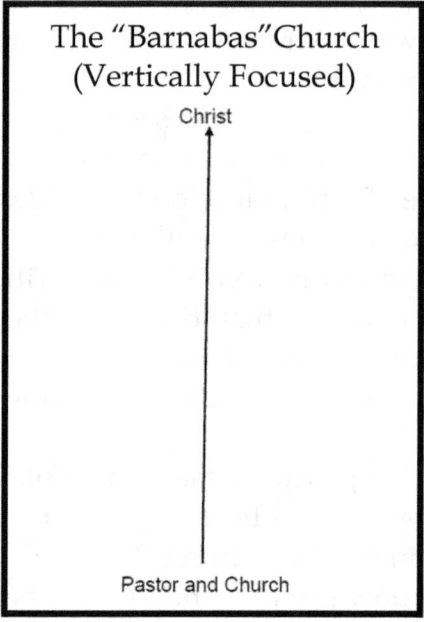

"Sam, to me this would have been the ideal church! The pastor and the church are fully devoted followers of Jesus Christ. Their sole purpose is to get to know *Him* better, to love *Him* more, and to move the spotlight away from each other and onto *Him*!"

"What's wrong with *that*, David?"

"Nothing in *theory*, Sam. Like there is nothing wrong in *theory* with Communism. It *sounds* like a good plan to share everything you have with the rest of the group, but it doesn't work in practice. Neither does the 'Barnaba Church.'"

"Why doesn't it work, David?"

"It doesn't work because we wouldn't be motivated to accomplish anything. Like Mary in the story in Luke 10, we Barnabas types would sit at His feet and learn more about Him. We would experience an emotional 'high.' We would love Him and each other more. That part would be great! But we wouldn't win many souls to Christ. And we also wouldn't do a very good job of assimilating new members."

"So what did you decide to do, David?"

"Once again, thanks for jumping into the boat, Sam. We decided to open door number three":

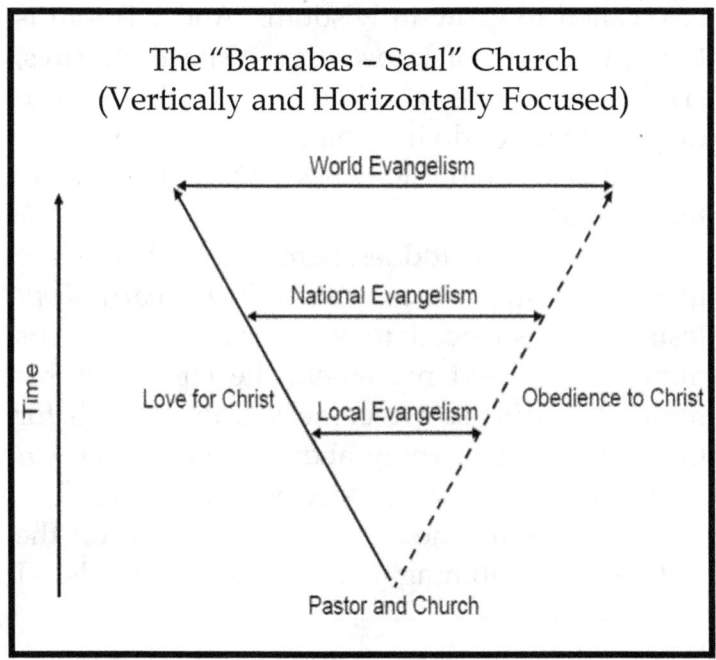

"As you can see Sam, the 'Barnabas – Saul' church combines the best facets of both the *Barnabas* and *Saul* churches.

It leaves out the limitations of both. The focus is no longer on people and performance, as in the *Saul* church."

I interject, "Praise the Lord for that!"

"Yes, Sam, praise the Lord for that! And the 'Barnabas – Saul' church also leaves out the spiritual navel gazing associated with the *Barnabas* church."

"But I *enjoy* the navel gazing, David."

"So do I Sam. But you and I weren't called to grow in our knowledge *alone*; we were also called to grow in wisdom. And wisdom is the application of knowledge. The Bible says, 'Therefore, to one who knows the right thing to do and does not do it, to him it is sin.'"[13]

I ask, tongue in cheek, "Does it *really* say that, David?"

"You *know* it does, Sam. And whether we like it or not, we need not only to learn *about* Jesus, we also need to walk *with* Him in His ministry." I nod my assent; he completes his thought. "And so we come *into* the church for the purpose of learning about Jesus, and go *out of* the church for the purpose of serving Him."

I have listened to David expound on the virtues of combining Barnabases and Sauls. I

---

[13] James 4:17.

understand his conclusions about the need to combine the two in a local setting. But I *cannot* accept the presence of a Saul in a Barnabas church. "David, how do you do it?"

"How do I do *what*, Sam?"

"For lack of a better word, 'harness' a working Saul so that he doesn't damage the church."

"That's a good point, Sam. I was concerned about that apparent dilemma, also. So I began to read about the Saul personality. Debi Stack wrote a book about Marthas—a.k.a., Sauls. She said:"

> *Like Martha, I am tempted to perfect my own personal kingdom, not seek the kingdom of God. Like Martha, I tend to view life as a series of projects, not a path toward knowing and serving Christ.*[14]

"Debi describes Saul's tendency to 'do' rather than to 'be.'"

I smile. "That's my point, David. Sauls are so busy working that they never take time to pray and to worship the Lord. And they *despise* those that do!"

---

[14] Debi Stack, <u>Martha to the Max: Balanced Living for Perfectionists</u>, Chicago: Moody Press, 2000, pg. 20.

"Right again, Sam. But we cannot let our personal feelings toward the Sauls in our lives cloud our judgment about God's ways of doing things. Debi Stack says in her next paragraph, 'And yet, the inherent perfectionistic Saul-qualities are there *by God's design* [emphasis added].'[15] In other words, the same God that made the Barnabases also made the Sauls. It's all about balance, Sam."

"Balance, David?"

"Yes, balance. Dr. Reginald Barnard was one of my favorite seminary professors. He often spoke of the 'balancing truths of the Word of God.' He said that, when people lean too far in one direction or the other, they will fall off of the tightrope of truth."

"Okay, David. Which truths?"

"I'm glad you asked, Sam. Once again you have jumped into the boat! One such truth is that God is both a God of love *and* a God of judgment. He is, in essence, a loving judge."

"Do you have any more, David?"

"I have a list of fifteen truths from the Bible that are, seemingly, contradictory":

1. Activity is rest.
2. Brokenness is wholeness.
3. Conflict is peace.
4. Death is life.

---

[15] Ibid.

5. Emptiness is fullness.
6. Fleeing is fighting.
7. Humble people are exalted.
8. Last is first.
9. Less is more.
10. Poverty is wealth.
11. Refugees are citizens.
12. Servants become rulers.
13. Slavery is freedom.
14. Surrender is victory.
15. Weakness is strength.

"Wouldn't such an exhaustive list be classified as 'overkill,' David?"

"Yes, it would, Sam. But we preachers certainly enjoy 'overkill,' don't we?"

"Maybe *you* do, David," I say playfully, "but *I* never would!" David smiles and gives a courtesy laugh. I continue, "So how does all this fit in with Sauls in the church?"

"Because, Sam, just as a church full of Sauls, like First Church, is out of balance, so a church full of Barnabases is also out of balance. God *made* both types of people, He *loves* both types of people, and He can *use* both types of people to accomplish His purposes in His church."

"So what is the secret, David? How can we blend the Barnabases with the Sauls without the Barnabases driving the Sauls crazy, and the Sauls trying to kill the Barnabases?"

"Sam, are you a bass this time? Or are you a carp? Welcome to the boat! I guess you would like to know the secret?"

"The secret, David?"

"Yes, Sam. The secret to combining the two groups under one roof."

"Oh, *that* secret? Yes I would."

Barnabas

"The secret, Sam, is fairly obvious—both Barnabases and Sauls need to be controlled by the Holy Spirit—hence the name, 'New Wine.' A Barnabas out of fellowship with the Lord can be just as destructive to the kingdom of God as a fleshly Saul."

I look at him askance. I say, "*Really*, David?"

"Yes really, Sam. I believe you are a *Barnabas*. Am I right?"

"Yes, thankfully, you are correct, David."

"And apparently you are *proud* of it," David says. He gives me the "I got you" look. He continues, "A backslidden Barnabas is the master of passive resistance (resistance especially to a government or an occupying power characterized mainly by noncooperation[16]). Let's check it out in the Bible. Turn to Matthew 21. Look at verses 28-32":

> *But what do you think? A man had two sons, and he came to the first and said, "Son, go work today in the vineyard." And he answered, "I will not"; but afterward he regretted it and went. The man came to the second and said the same thing; and he answered, "I will, sir"; but he did not go. Which of the two did the will of his father? They said, "The first." Jesus said to them, "Truly I say to you that the tax collectors and prostitutes will get into the kingdom of God before you. For John came to you in the way of righteousness and you did not believe him; but the tax collectors and prostitutes did believe him; and you, seeing this, did not even feel remorse afterward so as to believe him."*

"David, are you saying that the second son is a Barnabas?" He nods. I continue, "But I

---

[16] MERRIAM-WEBSTER'S COLLEGIATE DICTIONARY AND THESAURUS, DELUXE AUDIO EDITION®, Version 2.5, Copyright © Merriam-Webster, Incorporated, 47 Federal Street, P.O. Box 28l, Springfield, MA 01102.

thought the *disobedient* son must have been a Saul?"

"Sam, that's because you associate all of the negative traits with Saul and all of the positive traits with Barnabas. Sauls do not have the corner on the disobedience market! When a Barnabas Christian chooses to disobey God's will, he or she will agree on the *surface* to obey God, but then he or she will shut down. The bottom line is that a Barnabas will be just as likely to rebel against the Lord as a Saul."

"I guess you're right, David."

"Of course I am, Sam! And another thing: Mary used the identical wording as Saul in describing her unbelief. The Bible says, 'Martha then said to Jesus, "Lord, if You had been here, my brother would not have died."'[17] And, again, 'Therefore, when Mary came where Jesus was, she saw Him, and fell at His feet, saying to Him, "Lord, if You had been here, my brother would not have died."'"[18]

"So, David, are you claiming that Sauls are perfect, and that Barnabases are the real troublemakers in the church?"

"Of course not, Sam. I am saying that neither the Barnabases nor the Sauls are perfect!"

"Okay, David, okay, I understand!"

---

[17] John 11:21.
[18] John 11:32.

David resumes, "Debi Stack hit the nail on the head regarding Marthas—a.k.a., Sauls. She said":

> *Most of the time, we Marthas like things that fall into categories. A razor-sharp dividing line separates the right and the wrong, the "either" and the "or," the black and the white. Decisions are a snap. There's no agonizing over multiple solutions that could all be equally valid (as if!). Not only does rushing to judgment save time, it's the only form of exercise we get on most days.*

"Goliath," I exclaim. "I mean *Freddie*."

"Yes, Sam: Freddie. He has a 'one-size-fits-all' solution to disunity in the church: fire the preacher."

"And you wonder, David, why I don't particularly care for Sauls."

"No, I don't Sam. I don't much like them either. But if you and I will look closely, we will discover that even two Barnabases like us will have a little Saul lurking inside of our own lives."

"There is no way David!"

"Sam, to quote John Jacobs of the Power Team®, 'Yes way!' Didn't you tell me that you can be a cantankerous person when you have the upper hand?" I nod in affirmation. "And, given the same set of circumstances, wouldn't you have taken Freddie's same course of action?"

"David, you should have been a lawyer!"

"Yes Sam. Except for the fact that God has called me to be a preacher."

I think, "He must have called *David* to preach in self-defense!"

"So the secret, Sam, is to identify the characteristics of both the Spirit-filled Barnabas *and* the Spirit-filled Saul."

"Okay, David, what are they?"

He says, "Let's begin with the fruit of the Spirit":[19]

> *But the fruit of the Spirit is love, joy, peace, patience, kindness, goodness, faithfulness, gentleness, self-control; against such things there is no law.*

"Which of these characteristics do you think would particularly describe a Spirit-controlled Barnabas?"

Just to rile David up, I say, "*All* of them!" He knows I am joking.

"In a sense you're right, Sam. But, since the Holy Spirit is able to supernaturally transform the lives of believers, your answer, 'all of them' would also apply to Sauls. Let me ask

---

[19] Galatians 5:22-23.

the same question a different way: which of the attributes would be associated with a Saul?"

I respond, weakly, "*None* of them."

"Seriously, Sam, let's look at each one of the characteristics: love?" I shake my head. David continues, "Joy, peace, patience?" He continues down the list. I continue to shake my head, indicating my disagreement.

"So in other words, Sam, a Spirit-filled Saul would be much more easily identified than a Spirit-filled Barnabas?"

"That's right, David. Barnabases, by their very natures, are more likeable people."

"So, Sam—if the goal is to ensure that every church member is living a Spirit-filled Christian life, the Barnabases can pose an even greater threat to the life of a church than the Sauls."

"David, you surely know how to put a spin on your arguments. Are you sure you are not called to be an attorney?"

"I am an *advocate* for the Lord Jesus Christ!"

I think, "Whatever!"

"So as I said earlier, David, the secret is to identify the characteristics of a Spirit-filled Barnabas and a Spirit-filled Saul. So let's interact for a moment. Which prominent Bible character was known as Saul before he accepted Jesus Christ as his Lord and Savior?"

"That's easy—the Apostle Paul."

"'Ship ahoy,' Sam. I mean, 'Bingo.' Paul was a highly motivated, 'Type A,' personality. He invested all of his time and energies into moving up the Pharasaical ladder. He even attacked Christians, a group he believed to be a sect of his beloved Judaism. And what happened when Paul became a believer in Jesus Christ?"

I respond, "He gave the rest of his life in service to Jesus Christ. He started many new churches. He wrote the majority of the New Testament. Basically, his 'Saul' tendencies."

"Need I say more, Sam?"

"No, David."

He continues, "And now, Sam, we come to the difficult part. Name a Bible character that was a Barnabas before his or her salvation."

I begin to guess. "Peter?"

"No, Sam. Peter was definitely an overachiever. He answered questions before anyone else had the chance. He acted impetuously on more than one occasion. And he was a fisherman by trade. A Barnabas would have starved to death in that profession. Guess again."

"Okay, David. What about Jesus' mother, Barnabas? Wasn't she a Barnabas Christian?"

"Yes and no, Sam. She was acting like a Barnabas when the angel delivered God's message regarding the virgin birth to her: 'Behold, the bondslave of the Lord; may it be done to me according to your word.'[20] But she showed the determination of a Saul when she accompanied Jesus to the cross."

David's exposition regarding Jesus' mother has given me some time to ponder my next response. I shout, "I know the correct answer!"

"What is it, Sam?"

"Ruth! She left every*one* and every*thing* she knew in order to follow Naomi back to Israel. I remember her statement well. In fact, my daughter asked me to use it in her marriage ceremony":

> *Do not urge me to leave you or turn back from following you; for where you go, I will go, and where you lodge, I will lodge. Your people shall be my people, and your God, my God. Where you die, I will die, and there I will be buried. Thus may the Lord do to me, and worse, if anything but death parts you and me.*[21]

"I am way ahead of you, Sam! Ruth was, indeed, a Barnabas. But which personality type was *Naomi*?"

"I would guess that *she* was a Saul."

---

[20] Luke 1:38.
[21] Ruth 1:16-17.

"Right again, Sam. Listen to her discourse leading up to the verses that you have just quoted. Naomi says":

> *Return, my daughters. Why should you go with me? Have I yet sons in my womb, that they may be your husbands? Return, my daughters! Go, for I am too old to have a husband. If I said I have hope, if I should even have a husband tonight and also bear sons, would you therefore wait until they were grown? Would you therefore refrain from marrying? No, my daughters; for it is harder for me than for you, for the hand of the Lord has gone forth against me.*[22]

"Sam, doesn't Naomi sound a lot like a griping, whining, complaining Saul to you?"

"She surely does," I respond.

David smiles approvingly. "And yet which of the two women ultimately formulated the plan that united Boaz and Ruth in marriage?"

The light comes on for me. "Naomi did!"

"And Sam, did Boaz and Ruth have a baby?"

"Yes, David. His name was Obed. He was King David's grandfather."

---

[22] Ruth 1:11-13.

Partners in Planting

"That's good, Sam! And, of greater significance than being David's grandfather, Obed became an ancestor of our Lord Jesus Christ!"

I am wide-eyed at this point. David's understanding is becoming *my* understanding as well: we need both Barnabases *and* Sauls in our church!

David summarizes the Barnabas – Saul concept: "So the secret to the two types of Christians learning to coexist in a church, rather, ministering together in a church, is a mutual love and respect for each other. Do you think old, tired, worn out Naomi could have possibly attracted Boaz romantically?"

"No, David. I sincerely doubt that!"

"And was Ruth aware of the concept of the kinsman-redeemer?"[23] David answers his own question, "No, she wasn't. She was a foreigner!"

He is on a roll. "And did she know that demonstrating a servant's spirit would attract a wealthy man like Boaz?" He responds, "No! And can I get an 'Amen, Hallelujah!'"

I hold up my hand to stop his running homily. "So, David, are you telling me that a Naomi cannot function without a Ruth, and that a Ruth cannot function without a Naomi?"

---

[23] Deuteronomy 25:5-10.

"That's right, David. And Barnabas and Saul need each other. And you, my brother, need *Freddie!*"

I shudder at the thought. "Lord, help us, David! That would be like a story I once heard: a pastor had just moved to a new church in a different state. He soon discovered, a few weeks later, that the biggest troublemaker in his former church in the previous town had been transferred to the same town. And, not only that, the agitator and his family walked the aisle of his church at the end of a Sunday morning service in order to move their membership!"

"Sam, I am not talking about a *fleshly* Freddie. I am talking about a *Spirit-filled* Freddie." David reads my mind as he continues, "And no, that is *not* an oxymoron!"

"So how would I keep a Freddie in line?"

David hands an article to me that he found on the internet. He asks me to read it. I discover that the story has been written by some guy named, "Greg Atkinson." The footnote stated that Greg "has been writing, speaking, and training church leaders since 2000."[24] He

---

[24] http://www.thedisciplemakers.com/?cat=11, site visited on 6-1- 2011.

stated:[25]

Yesterday I took my son to the eye doctor because he had been complaining of having trouble reading things up close. He's getting reading glasses to wear just for homework and reading and will hopefully get better with time. As I sat in the room with him and watched them test his vision, I had a very interesting experience.

As they asked my son to read a chart up close, he began to mess up and couldn't focus on the letters. I sat there feeling helpless, uncomfortable, grieving and sincerely wishing he could do better. I left the doctor, dropped him back off at school and couldn't shake the feeling.

I started thinking about vision as it relates to leadership and what it must be like for people in a church where the leader lacks vision and there's nothing compelling about their mission. I wonder if they feel helpless, uncomfortable, if they grieve and sincerely wish the leader would make a call and lead them. The Bible says: "Where there is no vision [no redemptive revelation of God], the people perish"; PROVERBS 29:18 (Amplified

---

[25] http://gregatkinson.com/?s=%22no+vision%22, site visited on 6-1- 2011.

Bible).

I started thinking about that word PERISH. One of the definitions of PERISH is "to pass away or disappear" – I wonder if people in churches without vision die a slow death. I wonder how long they stick around feeling helpless, uncomfortable and grieving for their leader, their church and their community.

Yes, there are some people that quickly pick up on the lack of vision and leave the church to find another more vibrant church, but how many people keep coming back week after week secretly hoping things will get better? Hoping and praying that the pastor will get a word from God, lead with passion, conviction and purpose. I wonder how many gifted, capable, passionate lay leaders are sitting untapped in congregations around the country. I wonder.

"David, are you telling me in your sweet, loving, Barnabas way that the reason I had trouble with Freddie is that I didn't have a clear vision for First Church?"

David mutters something about the shoe fitting and somebody in this room having to wear it.

"Because," I continue, "if you *are*, you would be *exactly right*! I started my ministry at First Church with the vision of reaching the burgeoning community with the Gospel. I soon learned that very few people shared my vision. And the more I preached about it, the more resistant they became! The church, like many archaic institutions, suffered from an intense traditionalism and a resistance to change. I was never able to shift the direction of either the majority of the members or the leadership and, as a result, I guess I just conceded defeat."

"You're a typical Barnabas, Sam! That's why you need to be coupled with an atypical, Spirit-filled Saul. He, a *male* counterpart to Saul, will work with you in starting the new church. He will assist you in formulating a vision. He will hold you *accountable* for fulfilling that vision—just like Naomi did for Ruth."

"Are we talking about an *elder* system, David?"

"You will see, Sam; you will see. But here is a clue: "

> *Two are better than one because they have a good return for their labor. For if either of them falls, the one will lift up his companion. But woe to the one who falls when there is not another to lift him up. Furthermore, if two lie down together they keep warm, but how can one be warm alone? And if one can overpower him who is alone, two can resist him. A cord of three strands is not quickly*

torn apart.[26]

I think to myself, "A co-pastorate?"

David asks, "Are you ready to look at the training manual?"

"Yes David, I am."

"That's too bad, Sam! It's time for lunch!"

Steve's Instruction

David and I meet with Steve at the local steakhouse. David declares, "I'm buying!"

Those are magic words to a hungry and, for the better part of a year, an unemployed pastor!

After lunch we return to New Wine Church. David departs, as Steve begins: "Did you and David have a lot to talk about?"

"Yes, Steve, for the most part it was great. Some aspects of our conversation, however, seemed to be a little lopsided—in David's favor!"

"I know what you mean, Sam. David is really sharp. It's hard to win an argument, I mean, a *discussion*, with him!"

I think, "That's an understatement!"

---

[26] Ecclesiastes 4:9-12.

Steve says, "I guess you spent all morning talking about the Barnabas – Saul concept?"

"Yes, Steve. How did you know?"

"Because David and I have had that same discussion. And we have had it many times! And I thought, because of your situation with Freddie, you might be a little resistant."

"You're right, Steve. I was! But I now understand that David is right. Oh, and by the way — are you a Barnabas or a Saul?"

"Surprise, Sam! I am a full-blown, dyed in the wool, 100%, without question — Saul!"

I gulp as I think, "This is going to be tough!"

Steve continues, "And, as I'm sure you now realize, I am exactly what you need!"

"That remains to be seen, Steve."

Steve smiles, "And 'seen' it will be! I will become your drill-sergeant to whip you into shape! Several years ago, I heard a pastor use an illustration about drill-sergeants. I don't remember the exact wording but, at the end of our time together, you will be able to identify with these words from 'Old Sarge:'"

I am not your Momma. I don't care how you like your biscuits. I don't care how you slept last night. I do not wash your clothes and make your bed — you do. I will not come running to your side when you get hurt. And you'd better not ever talk back to me unless it is to say, "Yes, sir" and "no, sir."

What I will do for you is to make a man out of you. I will teach you how to fight and how to become a part of a unit. I will teach you how to survive on the battlefield. And, by the grace of God, I will bring you home.

"Sam, the good news is—you will only work with me for six months."

"What's the *bad* news, Steve?"

"The bad news is that my replacement will come to work with you at the end of the six months. And he is more of a Saul than I. Oh, and by the way, he will become your long-term ministry partner. What do you think about *that*, Sam?"

I calmly reply, "I guessed as much, Steve, as soon as David read that passage from Ecclesiastes chapter four!"

Steve continues, "Since you mentioned it, let's look again at Ecclesiastes chapter four. If you are like me, you have heard the other side of the argument, found in Luke 16:13":

No servant can serve two masters; for either he will hate the one and love the other, or else he will be devoted to one and despise the other. You cannot serve God and wealth.

"I have, Steve. A famous seminar leader used that verse to explain why partnerships don't work. The employees will side with one partner or the other, and the business will be divided."

"That's right, Sam. I heard the same thing. But let's look at the context. As Adrian Rogers used to say, 'a text without a context is a pretext'." Look at Luke 16:10-12:

> *He who is faithful in a very little thing is faithful also in much; and he who is unrighteous in a very little thing is unrighteous also in much. Therefore if you have not been faithful in the use of unrighteous wealth, who will entrust the true riches to you? And if you have not been faithful in the use of that which is another's, who will give you that which is your own?*

"What does *that* mean, Steve?" I ask.

"Sam, it means exactly what it says. It means that Jesus must be *the* Lord of your life. And, *if* He is *the* Lord of your life, He is also *the* Lord over your finances. And if He is *the* Lord over your finances, you will serve *Him* rather than your finances."

"I get that, Steve. So what does that have to do with a co-pastorate?"

"It has nothing to do with it at all. It means, Sam, that these verses cannot be used as an argument *against* it!"

"Okay, Steve, I understand. So, back to what you were saying about Ecclesiastes chapter four."

"Right, Sam. Ecclesiastes chapter four clearly teaches the need for a partnership in the ministry. Everyone struggles from time to time, and needs someone else to pick them up. We *all* want to throw up our hands and quit. *Especially* on Mondays!"

I laugh in agreement. Steve continues, "And so *if* we have a partner in the ministry — a co-pastor — we will have someone to pick us up when the challenges of the pastorate become too great for one person to bear."

I ask, "Isn't that what our wives are for? Aren't *they* our ministry partners?"[27]

"Yes and no Sam," Steve replies. Noticing my quizzical look, he continues, "In addition to having been your ministry partner, hasn't Rebecca always been one of your church *members*?"

"Of course, Steve," I answer.

"And doesn't she need to be ministered *to*, Sam?" I nod.

"And, Sam, wasn't she hurt more deeply than you were by your experience at First Church?" I nod again. My eyes well up with tears.

---

[27] Genesis 2:18.

Steve concludes, "And so, asking your wife to share the burdens of the ministry is really too much for her to bear. And, in my opinion, it is unfair of you to expect that level of sacrifice from her."

I think, "Steve really is a Saul. These Sauls can be so blunt. But they are also so correct!" I reply, "You're right, Steve. The pain Rebecca experienced was infinitely greater than my own personal pain. But I have a question for you."

"What is it Sam?"

"Since you and David are both advocating a co-pastorate, why don't either one of you have a ministry partner?"

"It's interesting that you should ask, Sam. Neither one of us has one right now. But we will *both* have one around the first of the year."

I venture an educated guess, "*You* are going to be David's Saul?"

"That's right, Sam. But I have been, in actuality, his Saul for years—on a consulting basis. We have been waiting for New Wine Church to grow to the point where they could support another full-time pastor. That time has now arrived. David and I are ready to make it official!"

"That's great, Steve!"

"Thanks Sam."

"I have another question, Steve."

"Yes Sam?"

"Who is *my* Saul?"

"You will see, Sam, in a few weeks. I will, however, give a clue to you: you already know the guy."

I think, "Some clue! And I have always hated the words, 'wait,' and 'we'll see.' But it seems that God particularly enjoys saying them to us! I know Steve well enough to know that I will just have to 'wait and see.'"

Fluke or Pattern?

Steve continues, "Sam, as you know, Mike Jackson from Faith Church will become one of your prayer partners. He will meet with us in about thirty minutes. I have asked him to tell you the story of his first ministerial position serving with William Morrison."

"Do you mean the pastor he worked with when he graduated from the seminary?"

"Yes, Sam. Has he told you much about his experience?"

"A little bit. Why?"

Steve shrugs his shoulders. He says, "I will let him tell you in his own words. Suffice it to say that Mike's story bears an amazing resemblance to the New Wine Strategy. Several churches have stumbled upon 'the Strategy' in times past. But, as far as we know, it has never previously been systematized. David and I believe it is really a principle, a gnomic truth, an aphorism. Have you ever read the book <u>Life is Tremendous</u>, by Charlie Jones?"

"Yes I have, Steve. It's a great book!"

"I agree, Sam. Charles 'Tremendous' Jones described seven principles that, he believed, could revolutionize our lives. He stated that the principles have been given to us by God Himself. Some well-meaning, good people never discover the principles and go through life as failures, while others stumble upon them by accident and are blessed. We believe the New Wine Principle, or Strategy, has been around for a long time. We, however, have identified the 'whys' and the 'hows' that will make it reproducible in other settings. Look at page 8 of the training manual. The heading for the chapter is, 'The Phenomenon of First Baptist Church of Jacksonville, Florida.'"

"That was an interesting story, Steve!"

"More than that, Sam—it is perhaps the best kept secret in recent church history. All of us 'preacher boys' thought that a co-pastorate would never work; something about the limitations of a partnership we learned about at that seminar you and I have attended. You know. Jesus said it in Luke 16:13":

> *No servant can serve two masters; for either he will hate the one and love the other, or else*

he will be devoted to one and despise the other. You cannot serve God and wealth.

We all sat around waiting for the church to collapse. It didn't. In fact, it grew tremendously! The website of First Baptist Church of Jacksonville, Florida, stated":

Another major turning point for First Baptist came in 1969 when the Pastor's son, Dr. Homer G. Lindsay, Jr. was called to the church as Co-Pastor. He would serve alongside his father until Dr. Lindsay Sr.'s retirement in 1975. From 1969 to 1988, Sunday school enrollment skyrocketed from 2,385 to 14,172. During this time nine buildings were either purchased or constructed, including the 3,500-seat Ruth Lindsay Auditorium (1976) and the Preschool Building (1986). [28]

I nod. "Okay, Steve, I can understand *that*. A father and son co-pastorate *might* work. And, the way I understood it, that was simply designed as a temporary, transitional, arrangement until Homer, Sr. retired."

Steve cannot contain his excitement. He says, "David and I thought the same thing, that

---

[28] http://www.fbcjax.com/about,site visited on 2-1 1-2012.

is, until we did some research. We found an out-of-print book by Belton S. Wall, entitled, A Tale to be Told. Wall stated, in plain terms":

> *Dr. Lindsay, Jr. had become accustomed to serving as co-pastor the three years he served with his father. When his father died in 1981, he felt the need for help in administering the affairs of a 12,000-member church. So in 1982, he approached his friend in the ministry, Dr. Jerry Vines, about becoming his co-pastor will all the rights and privileges of a pastor.[29]*

Dr. Lindsay, Jr. & Dr. Vines

I interrupt. "Steve, I am well aware of the fact that Dr. Lindsay and Dr. Vines shared a co-

---

[29] Belton S. Wall. A Tale to be Told: the History of the First Baptist Church of Downtown, Jacksonville. Jacksonville, FL: First Baptist, Jacksonville, 1999, p. 71.

pastorate. But how did their partnership work out?"

Steve is obviously elated by my question. He says, "Listen to the rest of the story":

> *Dr. Vines agreed and on July 4, 1982, assumed the role of co-pastor. It seems that this was a marriage made in heaven* [emphasis added]. *The coming of Dr. Vines provided an opportunity to expand the morning worship services to two sessions and thus prolong the need to construct a new auditorium. Dr. Vines has become a vital part in the planning, teaching, and preaching program of the church.*[30]

I enjoy playing the Devil's Advocate. I, smirkingly, say, "That is Wall's opinion. But do the facts substantiate his assertion?"

Steve is now, like David previously, about to *reel me in*. He continues, "The First Baptist website attested":[31]

> *In 1982, Dr. Jerry Vines joined Dr. Lindsay, Jr. as Co-Pastor and the miracles continued. In 1993, the congregation moved into its present auditorium which seats nearly 10,000.*

---

[30] Belton S. Wall. <u>A Tale to be Told</u>, p. 71.
[31] http://www.fbcjax.com/about, site visited on 6-1- 2011.

Partners in Planting

> *This magnificent worship center is a part of a church campus that covers more than nine city blocks. The most exciting part of this miraculous growth is that an average of 900 souls is saved and baptized into the First Baptist fellowship annually.*

I smile as I say, "Okay, Steve, you have convinced me. The Lord certainly used Dr. Lindsay, Jr. and Dr. Vines to work together to accomplish some amazing results. But what does that have to do with your Barnabas and Saul concept?"

"Sam, the things I am about to tell you are pure speculation, but here is what David and I have grown to believe: Homer, Sr. was a Barnabas pastor. His son, Homer, Jr., was a Saul pastor. Have you heard any stories about Homer, Jr.?"

"Oh yes, Steve. He was highly admired for his strong leadership abilities. A pastor friend of mine attended the First Baptist Church Pastors' Conference years ago. He said that Homer, Jr. noticed that one of the lights in the auditorium had burned out. This pastor told me that Homer, Jr. pointed at the ceiling and said, 'I see that a light bulb has burned out right there." Dr. Lindsay continued, "And, if it hasn't been replaced by tonight, somebody will be looking for a job!'"

"What happened next, Sam?"

I reply, "The pastor said the bulb had been replaced when they came back that night!"

Steve smiles, "I have another story."

"Tell me about it, Steve."

"Your story was *secondhand*, Sam — this one is *thirdhand*. It comes to me, via Mike Jackson, from William Morrison. William was visiting First Baptist, Jacksonville, on vacation. At the end of the service, Homer, Jr. called on Brother Smith, one of his deacons, to pray. Everyone bowed in prayer, but nothing happened. Homer, Jr. raised his head and, once again, asked Brother Smith to close in prayer. After another awkward period of silence, he said, 'Brother Smith, are you here? Has anyone seen Brother Smith?' And then he called on another man to pray."

I respond, "I guess Homer, Jr. must have thought Brother Smith was there in the service — I mean it *would* be difficult to pick one man out of such a large crowd."

"No, Sam. He *knew* Brother Smith was not there. But I can guarantee you one thing."

"What's that, Steve?"

"Brother Smith didn't miss another church service without letting his pastor know where he was going!"

"No, I'm sure he didn't, Steve!"

"And that is my point, Sam. Homer, Jr. was a *Saul* pastor!"

Partners in Planting

"I agree, Steve. But I am enjoying this. Do you have any more stories?"

"I do, Sam. Years ago my wife, Sarah, and I were attending a Southern Baptist Convention meeting. Dr. Jerry Vines was preaching. He told the story about his arrival as the new co-pastor of First Baptist Church. He was walking through the buildings when, off in the distance, he heard someone playing the drums. He followed the sound until he located the teenaged percussionist. Jerry introduced himself as the new pastor. And then he said, 'Young man, what do you think you are doing?' The reply, 'I'm playing the drums.' Jerry countered, 'I can see that, but I don't like the drums. So I want you to stop!'"

"What happened next, Steve?"

"He stopped playing, Sam. And Jerry walked happily away. But the story doesn't end there. Apparently the young man had the opportunity to speak to Dr. Lindsay. Homer, Jr. summoned Dr. Vines into his office. He asked Jerry to close the door. He said, 'Jerry, you are without a doubt the finest preacher I have ever heard, and we are thrilled to have you here working with us. But let's get one thing straight: First Baptist Church has only one final authority—and it's not *you*.'"

"What did Jerry say, Steve?"

"He just looked puzzled. Homer, Jr. continued, 'I understand that you told one of our teenagers you don't particularly like to hear the drums being played during a worship service.' Jerry replied, 'That's right, I did.' Homer, Jr. continued, 'Well I *do* like the drums. Do we understand each other?' Jerry snapped to, with military precision, as he said, 'Yes, *sir!*'"

"And then, Sam, he quipped to those of us in attendance at the Convention hall, 'And do you know what? I *immediately* started to like the drums, too!' The entire room erupted in laughter, especially those of us that had previously heard about Homer, Jr.'s reputation!"

Steve and I chuckle together as we consider the implications of the statement Homer, Jr. made to Dr. Vines.

Mike Jackson walks in. He says, "Hello Steve and Sam. What is so funny?"

Steve answers, "I was just telling Sam about the 'drum incident' between Dr. Homer Lindsay, Jr. and Dr. Jerry Vines."

"Oh, that is funny," Mike says. "Was that designed to be a lead-in to my experience with William Morrison?"

"No, Mike, but it *could* be."

Mike begins, "Okay, Steve." He looks at me as he continues, "Sam, Steve has already heard this story, but I am sure he won't mind hearing it again. Will you, Steve?" Steve smiles and shakes his head. Mike continues, "Sam, I was fresh out of the seminary. I think I have already told you about the way I was called to serve at Mountain Springs Church by Brother William, the committee of one."

"I *do* remember that, Mike."

"Great, Sam. Here is how my time at Mountain Springs fits into the 'New Wine Strategy.' As you might have guessed, Brother William was the Saul pastor and I was the Barnabas pastor."

I say jokingly, "No, *really*, Mike! I thought that *you* were the Saul and *Brother William* was the Barnabas!"

Mike grins as he continues, "There was no doubt in anyone's mind that Brother William was the person in charge at Mountain Springs. Everyone both *adored* and, simultaneously, *feared* him. None of us dared to question his authority. But we all knew one thing…"

"What's that, Mike?" I ask.

"We all knew that Brother William walked with God. That he loved Jesus with all of his heart, and that he loved the people of the community and the church."

I respond, "What a man! You were privileged to have worked with him!"

Mike continues, "I was, Sam. And without being boastful, he was also privileged to have worked with me."

I smile but, as I read Mike's body language, I realize he is being serious. "How so, Mike?"

"Sam, Brother William was one of the finest soul-winners I have ever met. He inspired me to join him in that venture. During my second year at Mountain Springs, we baptized 105 people into the membership of the church!"

I respond, "105?!"

"That's right, Sam. And we baptized more than 100 the next year, also!"

"That's great, Mike!"

"Yes it is Sam. And years later, after I left Brother William to become the senior pastor of another church, Brother William and the members of Mountain Springs Church continued to have outstanding baptismal years!"

"So what was the secret, Mike?" I ask.

"The secret was the New Wine Strategy! Two pastors, one a Saul and the other a Barnabas, guided by the leadership of God's Holy Spirit, loving each other and the people, and reaching out in order to win the community to Jesus Christ." Mike looks wounded as he says, "But they must *both* be controlled by the Spirit."

Noticing Mike's falling countenance, I remark, "What happened, Mike?"

"Sam, as I said, I went to my first church as the senior pastor. I tried to *be* Brother William, but I *wasn't*. I couldn't get up early in the morning to pray—I would just fall asleep. I couldn't give half my income back to the church—I was serving as the pastor of a mission

Partners in Planting

church on a very limited salary. I could, however, share my faith with lost people, and I *did*. Every day, from 8:00 in the morning until 10:00 every night."

"I would guess that you won a lot of people to Christ?"

"My wife told me she believed it was more than 200 in four years."

"That's wonderful, Mike!"

"Yes, it is. And no, it *wasn't*, Sam. I almost lost my family. Brother William, as a Saul pastor, was Superman®. He could balance the time with his family and his time with the church. I *couldn't*. I never managed to find the time I should have been spending with my kids as they were adjusting to a new environment. I missed a lot of meals with my family. The church ultimately became my life."

"What happened next, Mike?"

"I made another poor decision. I began dialoguing with Brother William about the possibility of returning to Mountain Springs. He was elated! He said, 'Mike, I would love to have you back!' And the people of Mountain Springs agreed. I received a 100% vote to return. I later asked Brother William, 'Do you know what that 100% vote tells me?' Brother William replied, 'What's that, Mike?' I said, 'That tells me that *somebody* didn't vote!' We both laughed, because we both knew that I was right."

"So, Mike, you went back to Mountain

Springs?"

"I did, Sam. But this time I had also developed some Saul characteristics of my own: I no longer was an innocent Barnabas. I no longer complemented Brother William. And we were no longer the 'Dynamic Duo.' Sam, it was seven years of misery for both of us! I finally left the church with feelings of resentment toward Brother William." Mike starts to cry.

Steve places his hand on Mike's shoulder. He assures him, "It's okay, Mike. I remember the time I wept in front of one of my seminary professors. He said, 'My daddy used to tell me that men don't cry. My daddy was wrong. I believe it takes a real man to know how to cry.' So you go right ahead, Mike."

Mike slowly regains control. He says, "I'm sorry guys. It's just that I believe Brother William was in tune with the Lord in asking me to return to Mountain Springs. On my part, I was not in tune with the Lord in the *way* I went back. If I could have exercised 20-20 hindsight, I would have known that the real problem was not with Brother William. It was with *me*."

I step in, "So how did it all work out, Mike?"

"I later apologized to Brother William. He told me he had already forgiven me. And I knew that he had. But the kingdom of God lost a great team when Brother William and I parted ways. We could have had another great

Partners in Planting

ministry together. But, now, that is no longer possible. Brother William is in poor *physical* health and I am a *spiritual* wreck!"

"I am so sorry, Mike."

"That's okay, Sam. If my personal failures can help you to succeed, then the pain and suffering have all been worthwhile." He winks. "And, maybe, in the process we can find another pastor like Brother William to work with *me*."

"I will be praying for you, Mike."

Mike grins, "No, Sam. I am *your* prayer partner. *I* will be praying for *you*!"

"Okay, Mike," I reply.

Steve says, "Men, let's stop talking about praying and just do it."

And, for the next hour, that is exactly what we do.

Debriefing Time

Having concluded my meeting with Steve and Mike, I return home to Rebecca. She asks, "How was your day, dear?"

I reply, "Very *long* and very *productive*."

"Productive?" she asks.

"Yes. I found out that I am not going to be the *only* pastor of the new church."

Rebecca places her cell phone on the

counter (she loves FaceBook™). She gives her full attention to me. "Sam, do you mean that the church will have multiple pastors?"

"It's not *that* bad, Rebecca. It will only have *two*."

And then I explain the New Wine Strategy to her: that the new church will be led by a Saul pastor and me (the Barnabas pastor). She seems skeptical at first but, as I tell her the stories of Homer Lindsay, Jr. and Jerry Vines, and of Mike

Foster and William Morrison, I can see she begins to both *understand* and *accept* the premise.

Since lunch has now run its course, I change the subject by asking, "What's for supper?"

I receive the dreaded reply, "Your favorite: leftovers!"

*I force a half-smile. "That's *great*, Rebecca."

She replies, "Nothing but the best for my conquering hero!"

Saul

My name is Todd Williams. My wife, Lisa, and I have been married for ten years and

Partners in Planting

have three children. I will become the "Saul" of the co-pastorate with Sam Anderson.

I am several years younger than Sam, but I have grown to respect him. Lisa and I were formerly members of First Church. Sam was our pastor, and a good one! We were devastated when First Church forced him to resign. No *pastor*—let me rephrase that. No *Christian*, rather, no *dog* should have been subjected to the things Sam and Rebecca have suffered at the hands of a group of *so-called* Christian brothers and sisters. But Sam says that it has been worth it. That he has learned more about mercy through the experience than he has ever known. What a guy!

Sam, Lisa, and I have been on a few international mission trips together, and have enjoyed working together on a short-term basis. Lisa and I are both prayerful and hopeful that we can maintain a successful long-term ministerial relationship with Sam and Rebecca.

I am considered by many to be a successful businessman. I also have a seminary degree. Unlike Sam, I will be financially able to underwrite my own ministerial expenses for the first two years.

I have a meeting this morning with my two future trainers: David Hanson and Steve Caldwell. I have spoken with David on numerous occasions. He is the pastor that has asked me to pray about this new venture. I think Steve may also be a pastor, or some other leader in a church. I am not really sure.

David begins, "Todd, thank you for meeting with us this morning. This is Steve Caldwell, pastor of Trinity Church."

I think, "So, Steve *is* a pastor." That answers my question.

David continues, "He has been our Saul, your counterpart, at New Wine Church for the last two years. He will officially join our staff in January."

I extend my hand. "Hello, Steve. It's nice to meet you."

Steve reciprocates, "And it's nice to meet you, too. David and I are both thrilled to have a man of your caliber on board with us!"

I quip, "I'm sorry, Steve. Are you talking about *Sam*, or about *me*?" They both laugh.

David resumes his discourse. "There is no need for false modesty, Todd. Steve and I are both aware that you have a long record of achievement as a successful Christian businessman." David points to himself as he says, "And we Barnabases always appreciate godly Sauls!"

"Thank you, David," I respond. "And we Sauls also appreciate godly Barnabases."

Steve reenters the conversation. "Stop it, you two! This 'Mutual Admiration Society' is going to make me sick!" David and I laugh.

I take the lead. "Men, I have read through the Training Manual. You have done a superb job in preparing Sam and me for the new church start. I especially appreciate the additional information written in italics—Steve, I believe you are responsible for that." Steve smiles broadly. I have won him over.

"Thank you, Todd," Steve says. "I have found that it has been almost impossible to improve upon the great work that David, here, has done."

David retorts, "Now *I* am going to be sick!" Steve and I laugh.

I continue, "I hope you two don't mind, but I have made a few revisions of my own. You may want to incorporate them as an underlined text, should you decide to include them in your Manual."

Steve and David exchange glances. David winks. And then he and Steve give one another the "high five." Steve says, "Thank you for 'jumping into the boat.'"

I ask, "What is that supposed to mean?"

"It means," Steve says, "your willingness to make revisions to the manual is *exactly* what David and I have been praying that you would want to do! We are both aware that one person cannot possibly see all of the angles in a new venture. We are thrilled that you have given us your input—and we know it will be tremendous!"

I respond, "Oh, *I* see, Steve. What you mean is that the fish has jumped into the boat. You two didn't even have to reel me in."

"You're sharp, Todd," David says. He glances at Steve as he continues, "I believe we have *definitely* found the right man for the job!" Steve nods in agreement.

David proceeds: "Todd, just as Steve and I will both be working with Sam over the next few months, we will also be working with you. You will likely learn more from me, since I am the Barnabas pastor at New Wine. Similarly, Sam will learn more from Steve. We will major on the similarities you and Sam to understand the differences."

I am growing a little restless. And, being a Saul, I make no attempt to hide it. Steve, astutely, picks up on it. "Listen, Todd, we know you need to get back to the office. May we pray with you?"

"Sure, Steve," I reply. We pray together for a few minutes. The meeting is adjourned.

The Office

I know that God must be at work, because the devil has *really* been on the attack. It seems that everything at my office has been going crazy! My secretary walks in. I glance up from a

Partners in Planting

stack of accounting figures that indicate our company's profit curve is moving southeast. "Yes, Karen?"

"Mr. Williams, I am sorry to interrupt you."

"What is it, Karen?"

"Mr. Simmons, I mean, Harold, wants to see you in his office."

Harold is the C.E.O.[32] of the company. He is a Saul on steroids. "Thank you, Karen. I am on my way there right now."

I walk down a short corridor, and into Harold's outer office. He has the "Big Office Syndrome." He has assigned himself the corner office on the top floor of our building. I have never *seen* so many windows. His secretary, Michelle, smiles and asks me to sit down for just a minute.

"A minute," I think. "Harold loves to make people wait so that he can have the upper hand in a meeting."

"He will see you now," Michelle informs me.

I walk in. Harold also has the "Big Chair Syndrome." You know: the leather chair that rises majestically three feet above the crown of his severely balding head. And the chairs on the other side of his highly polished, imported, genuine mahogany desk were designed for very

---

[32] Chief Executive Officer

short people. You never enter this sanctum without realizing that *he* is the boss.

Harold rises. He is wearing a well-rehearsed smile. He motions to one of the miniature chairs on the far side of his desk. I mutter, "He has the 'Big Desk Syndrome,' too. "

"Please have a seat," he says.

I perform as instructed. "What's on your mind, Harold?"

His smile quickly fades. His brow becomes deeply furrowed. I have the gift of discernment: Harold is concerned. "Have you seen these financials?" he asks.

I reply, "I was looking at them when you summoned me."

"Then you know, Todd, they are in a steep decline!"

"Yes, sir."

"And you also know that, as our C.F.O.,[33] they are primarily *your* responsibility." I nod. He continues, "What are you going to do about it? I have a board meeting this afternoon, and the members are going to want some favorable answers."

I smile, gratuitously. "I have it covered. I am firing the sales manager later this morning."

Harold feigns a look of concern. "Tom? He seems like a nice guy."

"He *is*, Harold. But being a nice guy

---

[33] Chief Financial Officer

Partners in Planting

won't put our company on top. Do you remember what Harry Truman always said?"

"Yeah," Harold replies. "The buck stops here."

"That's right, Harold. So you can tell the board members that we will be replacing Tom — with Greg Watson."

"Isn't Greg our top *salesman*?"

"Yes, Harold, but he is much more than that. He is also a team player. I have sent him out on calls with some of our newer salespeople. They always seem to come back with a sale. As you and I both know, Greg is the one that closes the deals. And yet Greg *always* splits the commission!"

Harold continues, "He sounds like he might be our guy!"

"I am sure of it, Harold."

He stands. He reaches across his desk. He doesn't shake my hand, but he points his finger just inches away from my nose. He says, "You'd better be. In this case, the buck stops right *there*, with *you*. *I* have nothing to do with this decision!"

"Okay, Harold. Do you have anything else?" He shakes his head. "No, that's all."

I leave Harold's office. I think, No wonder they call him, "Teflon™ Harold." What an appropriate nickname. Nothing sticks to him!

The Difficult Part of My Job

I return to my office. Karen reads by my facial expression that I am concerned about something. "Is anything wrong, Mr. Williams?" she asks.

Without thinking, I prevaricate. I tell a lie. "No, Karen. Everything is fine. Would you contact Tom Harrison? Ask him to come to my office ASAP."[34]

"Okay, Mr. Williams. Will there be anything else?"

"No, Karen, that's all."

I sit, somewhat dejectedly, behind my desk. All of the chairs in my office, including mine, are of the same style and size. They are the typical swiveled, burgundy-colored office chairs of the cloth, not leather, variety. My philosophy, unlike Harold's, is that, when you truly are a big man, you don't have to let anyone else know it.

Karen buzzes in on the intercom: "Mr. Harrison is here to see you."

I reply, "Send him in."

---

[34] As soon as possible.

Partners in Planting

Tom walks in. He glances around the room. His eyes fall upon the stack of financials strewn across the top of my inexpensive, particle board desk. He knows. But we will still go through the process.

"Have a seat," I say, as I move around to sit next to him in one of the empty chairs located at the front of my desk. My policy has always been to treat everyone that comes through my office door with respect. I deliberately place myself on the same level with them. There are no artificial boundaries or "home court advantages" in *my* office. Tom, warily, sits.

"What is it, Todd?" he asks. He corrects himself, "I mean, Mr. Williams?"

"I think you know, Tom. Our sales have dropped dramatically over the last quarter."

Tom shows several telltale signs of nervousness: he can't look me in the eye. Beads of sweat literally begin to form on his now colorless forehead. He fidgets in his chair. He continues, "But I have this new sales plan..."

I stop him in mid-sentence. "Don't embarrass yourself, Tom. You and I both know you have had a 'new sales plan' every quarter for the last two years. And, until now, your plan has been fairly successful. This time, however, it has failed."

He resorts to groveling. Through pleading eyes, he says, "Please don't fire me,

Todd! I have a kid in college and my wife is sick. I *need* this job!"

As a Saul, I have a problem with compassion. Or, rather, a *lack* of it. Seeing Tom on his knees, begging for his job, really doesn't have any effect on me at all. "Tom, I am sorry." (I'm not *really* sorry, but H.R.[35] says I have to say it). I continue, "I am going to have to let you go."

I retreat to my side of the desk. I open the middle drawer and remove an oversized manila envelope. I extend the packet across the desk to him. I give him my well-rehearsed spiel: "You will find that we are going to take good care of you and your family. We will give you a good reference to your potential employers. We will also give you six months' pay as severance, along with all of your insurance benefits and profit-sharing contributions. Finally, our H.R. department is offering to provide you with career placement counseling to help you find another job."

Tom's countenance noticeably changes. He is no longer nervous. I believe he is now experiencing feelings of both anger and betrayal.

"Todd," he says, "I thought you and I were friends!"

---

[35] The Human Relations Department of the company.

Partners in Planting

"We are, Tom. And I hope our friendship will continue. We just won't be *working* for the same company."

I extend my hand toward his. He stares furiously at my hand, a hand that he refuses to shake. I have never previously heard Tom use profanity, but I hear it now! He storms out of my office door. He slams it shut behind him. The glass rattles. I walk across the room and open the door. I look as he proceeds through the expanse of my outer office.

Karen, inconveniently, says, "Have a nice day, Mr. Harrison."

He looks back at her. He says, "Yeah, right!" And then he slams *her* door.

Karen turns her attention to me. She asks, "Is Mr. Harrison having a bad day, Mr. Williams?"

"You could say that, Karen. You could say that."

I pivot on my left foot to return to my office. As an afterthought, I glance over my right shoulder. I ask, "Karen, would you mind doing me a big favor?"

She responds, "Certainly not, Mr. Williams. What is it?"

"Make a lunch appointment for me with Greg Watson."

"Where would you like to meet him, Mr. Williams?"

"I will let you pick a nice local restaurant, Karen. I really don't care."

"Okay, Mr. Williams," Karen says, as she picks up the phone and speed-dials Greg's number.

I smile and slowly close my door.

Lunch with Greg

Greg and I meet at a four-star restaurant located two blocks from our corporate offices. We engage in the usual small talk. We discover that our families are both fine, and the kids are still growing—blah, blah, blah.

I ask, "Greg, I suppose that you have already heard about Tom?"

"I did, Mr. Williams."

I wave my hand in an effort to correct him. I say, "Todd. Call me Todd."

"Okay, *Todd*. I *have* heard about Greg. We folks down in sales were all shocked! He seemed like a great guy. I thought that he was really on top of things."

The typical Saul, I get right to the point. "Well, Greg, he *wasn't*. And that's why I have asked you to meet with me today."

Now Greg looks worried. "Have *I* done something wrong, Mr. Williams? I mean, Todd."

"No Greg, you haven't done anything wrong. You have done something *right*. In fact, you have done *many* things right."

He responds, "Then what is it? Why are we meeting today?"

"I want you to take Tom's position as sales manager."

He is genuinely surprised. "You want *me* to be the sales manager?"

"That's right, Greg. You have all of the qualities I am looking for in a person to fill this position."

Greg looks dumbfounded. "I do?"

"Yes, Greg. You are extremely patient when you are working with the new guys. You even show them the ropes at your own personal expense."

Greg explains, "I'm only doing what any of the other guys would do."

I challenge his statement. "That's not true, Greg. You are much too modest." And then it dawns on me. Greg Watson is a Barnabas! He is a relational person. He loves people, and wants to help them to succeed. No wonder I like him! I realize something else: this can become a part of my training regimen for working with Sam in the new church start.

"Listen, Greg," I continue, "you have all of the qualities I am looking for in a manager." Greg looks skeptically at me. I continue, "And I know what you're thinking."

"What am I thinking, Todd?" he asks.

"You think you would be getting yourself way in over your head."

"You're right. I *do*, Todd. May I have a few days to think about it, and to talk it over with my wife?"

I say, "Greg, you don't have to use your code language with me. I am well aware that you are a Christian. And I know that you are *really* asking for time to pray about it, aren't you?"

"Yes, I am, Todd. I never make any major decisions without consulting 'the Boss.'"

"Greg, I wouldn't have it any other way. How soon can you let me know?"

"Can I give you my answer on Monday, Todd?"

"That's fine, Greg. I will be praying *with* you and *for* you."

Greg's expression changes to one of surprise. He asks, "Are you a Christian too, Todd?"

I think, "The hazards of being a Saul." I reply, "Yes, Greg, contrary to popular opinion!" We laugh together as I pay the bill.

The Meaning Behind the Meeting

The following Monday morning I get up at my customary 5:00. I go to the exercise room. I distractedly go through my daily routine. I check my agenda to make sure I have a handle on my day.

After my shower, I spend thirty minutes, alone, in prayer. "What are You telling me, Lord?" I ask.

As a Saul, I am naturally impatient. Thirty minutes of silence nearly *killed* me in the beginning. But I have learned that there is nothing on my mind of which Jesus isn't already aware. So, instead of running through my shopping list of prayer requests, I have just learned to sit and listen. And, believe it or not—and many Christians *don't*—God speaks.

Today I have a powerful awareness that He agrees with my choice of Greg Watson as sales manager. But then I have a caution in my spirit: I had better not mistreat him. In fact, the Lord wants me to learn to have more compassion for, and loyalty to, both my subordinates and my superiors.

I interrupt the Lord for just a minute. "*Superiors*, Lord?" But I know what He means. I spend the next five minutes confessing my wrong attitudes toward Harold. I will have to learn to love him unconditionally, just the way he is (God *already* does), if I am *ever* going to have the opportunity to share my faith in Jesus Christ with him.

I return to listening mode. He explains the sensitive nature of a Barnabas. I object. "Lord, did you see how Sam took all of that abuse? Barnabases are *not* sensitive!"

The Lord explains to me that He had given Sam the grace he needed to handle the situation, and how Sam learned more about mercy through his affliction.

I respond with one of the most foolish things we Christians say in prayer: "You're right, Lord." And then I ask Him what He wants for me to do.

He explains that I am to trust Greg explicitly. And I am to "watch his back." The other salesmen with more tenure will be trying to undermine his authority. Contrary to his feigned indifference, our C.E.O., Harold, will be scrutinizing his every move!

Greg's Decision

Greg is waiting in my outer office when I arrive. "Could I speak with you for a minute, Todd?"

"Sure, Greg. Why don't you come on in?"

We walk into my office together. I sit in my usual "low authority" spot. Greg sits next to me. I ask, "What is it, Greg?"

"I have decided to accept your offer, Todd," he says.

"That's great, Greg," I exclaim.

He holds up one finger as he cautions, "But with one caveat."

"What's that, Greg?"

"That I don't have to fire anybody! I just couldn't do that!"

"Yes you could, Greg. But I will help you. I will follow the coaching model of John Maxwell." I hand Greg a sheet of paper, with the heading, "Maxwell's Model":[36]

Maxwell's Model:

1. I do it. I terminate the first round of salesmen.
2. Ii do it, and you watch. You observe as I terminate the second round of salesmen.
3. You do it, and I watch.
4. You do it (all by yourself).

---

36 http://smartleadersnetwork.com/2011/01/12/lessons-learned-from-john-maxwell-part-2/, "Let Your Leaders Fly for a While," site visited on 6-5-2011.

Greg asks, "Just what exactly does that mean, Todd?"

"As I am sure you have learned, Greg, I don't have a problem with terminating an employee."

He laughs. "You can say *that* again!" I join in the laughter, but I stop abruptly. Greg also stops.

I continue, "According to step number one, I will handle the first round of terminations in the sales department. You probably have two or three employees that need to be fired right now."

"I do, Todd. So you are going to handle it?"

"That's the deal, Greg." He breathes a sigh of relief. I continue, "But the next round I will do it and you will be present in the meeting. You won't have to *say* anything. I just want you to watch."

"So far, so good, Todd."

"And that's where it all ends, Greg. The third round belongs to you. You handle the terminations while *I* watch."

Greg begins to fidget again. He says, "So I guess I had better get rid of *everybody* in my department by the end of round two!"

"No, Greg. But here is the good news: once you have learned how to conduct a termination, you will be able to handle your employees with much more compassionate than I ever could!"

"I don't know about that, Todd."

"*I* do, Greg. Do you remember Barnabas and Saul in the Bible?" He nods his head. And then I launch into a ten minute briefing about the differences.

"Wow, Todd," Greg says. "Last week I was surprised to learn that you were a *Christian*. Now I find out that you actually study your Bible!"

I lean forward as I say, in muffled tones, "Don't tell anybody Greg, but I also have a seminary degree. I have considered going into the ministry."

Greg's jaw literally drops. "I surely wouldn't have guessed that!" he says. And then he apologizes for his callousness.

"No need to do that, Greg. I don't always *act* like a Christian when I am here at work. That's where *you* can help *me*."

"You want *me* to help *you*, Todd?"

"Yes, Greg. I am about to enter into a co-pastorate with my former pastor, Sam Anderson."

Without thinking, he blurts, "Oh, you are going to be working with that *loser*."

Note to self: Barnabases are not always nice to other Barnabases, just as Sauls are not always nice to other Sauls. I rise to Sam's defense, "That 'loser,' as you put it, is a great man of God! He has suffered for the cause of Christ! I am honored to have the privilege of working with him in starting a new church!"

"Slow down Todd," Greg says. "I spoke before I had a chance to think. It's just that the word around my Christian circles is that he deserved everything that happened to him."

"Greg, as I'm sure you understand, there is no such thing as *Christian* gossip. Gossip, by any other name, is simply gossip. Even when it has been carefully couched as a prayer request."

"You're right, Todd. I want *you* to forgive me. And I will also ask *the Lord* to forgive me. How can I help?"

"You will teach me the way in which a Barnabas would deal with various situations. That will help me to better understand Sam."

"You've got it, boss! I mean, Todd."

"Thanks, Greg."

The Formation of a Partnership

I, Sam, have been feverishly speculating as to the identity of *my* Saul. After three months of training, David, Steve, and I are *finally* going to meet together with him.

Partners in Planting

One of my former church members, Todd Williams, walks into the room. I speak. "Hello, Todd. What are *you* doing here?"

"Haven't they told you?" Todd asks, as he looks first at David and then at Steve.

"Told me what, Todd?"

"That *I* am your Saul, Sam."

"*You* are, Todd? I had no idea."

Todd grins as he continues, "I am sorry to disappoint you!"

"Oh, I am not *disappointed*. In fact, I am *overwhelmed*!"

Todd looks at me, quizzically. "*Overwhelmed*, Sam?" he asks.

"Yes, Todd, I really am! David and Steve could not have possibly picked a better co-pastor to lead our new church. You and Lisa were among the few people that left First Church immediately after the incident. Mind, you I haven't been disappointed by those that chose to stay—they did what they, at the time, believed to be right."

Todd nods in agreement. He asks, "I guess you have heard about the trickling 'mass exodus' that has occurred over the last several months."

"Yes, I have," I continue. "But I truly admire the people, like you and Lisa, who promptly took a stand and moved to other places. I am, indeed, *overwhelmed*!"

Todd says, "And so am I, Sam. Lisa and I are both honored to have been given this privilege of working with you and Rebecca in the new ministry. I know that the Lord is in it, and that the four of us will make a wonderful team!"

David reenters the conversation. "Here we go again—another 'Mutual Admiration Society.'"

Todd comes to the rescue. "The only downside, Sam, is that we have to work with *these* two clowns. I hope they don't quit their day jobs!"

"Touché, Todd," Steve says. "We will leave you guys alone to discuss your plans." He and David leave the room.

Meeting Again

"Well, Sam," Steve asks, "how is everything at the Anderson house?"

"Things are going great, Todd. How are Lisa and the kids?"

"All fine. Steve and David have really put us through the mill, haven't they?"

"*Tell* me about it, Todd. I almost quit two months ago!"

"Did you really, Sam?"

"I really did, Todd. Steve told me that his nickname was 'Old Sarge.' He wasn't kidding! I have just been through some sort of spiritual boot camp!"

"Well, I'm glad you *didn't* quit. I believe the Lord has great things in store for all of us as we begin this new venture."

"I do, too, Todd. Are you ready for the team training?"

"I'm as ready as I will ever be, Sam."

"Then let's go meet with David and Steve so we can get things started."

The Overview

Todd and I walk down the hall to David's office. We find Steve and David doing what preachers do best: eating doughnuts and drinking coffee. Someone has rightly called coffee "Christian gasoline." We can't go anywhere without it. "Hello, guys," I say, "Did you save us any (referring, primarily, to the doughnuts)?"

David replies, "We bought two dozen. I think there may be a couple of the plain ones left." I mutter my disapproval.

We eat doughnuts and carry on a meaningless conversation, everything from the weather to our favorite ball teams. Coffee break is over and the work begins! We move into an empty classroom.

We discover two unexpected guests—Lisa and Rebecca. Todd speaks. "What are you fine-looking ladies doing here?" I think, "What a schmoozer!"

The six of us—Todd, Lisa, David, Steve, Rebecca, and I—spend the next hour talking about the need for loyalty and acceptance.

Loyalty

Part One

Steve tells Todd and me that he and David have invited our wives to participate in our discussion on the need for "loyalty."

"Loyalty?" I ask. "Do you think we are going to have a problem with loyalty?"

Steve affirms, "We are sure that you *won't*, at least in the beginning. But you wait until the church begins to grow."

"I thought that was the idea?" Rebecca asks.

"It *is*," Steve replies. "As the new members begin to join the church, and we know they will, you will have all sorts of people from various backgrounds. The majority of those that will join will love both Sam and Todd, but some will naturally gravitate to one of them above the other. And others will try to gain power in the church by turning one of them against the other."

Lisa speaks, "I understand. Todd and I have three kids. They have already learned that I am more likely to say 'Yes' than is Todd. And so they try to bypass him as frequently as possible." "Right, Lisa," Steve says excitedly. Evidently Sauls appreciate the insights of Barnabases. Oh, and not so surprisingly, Lisa is a Barnabas. Isn't it funny how opposites attract?

David is a little stingier with his praise. "So, Lisa, how do you handle that in your home?"

Lisa replies, "Todd and I didn't know what to do at first. But we have learned, through experience, to tell the kids to wait until we have a chance to discuss the matter together. And, because the Bible teaches that family comes before career, Todd has given me permission to call him at work when I need his input."

And now a Barnabas demonstrates his appreciation of the wisdom of another Barnabas. "Outstanding, Lisa," David replies. He continues, "And that is exactly the way your husbands need to handle similar situations as they arise in the new church."

I chime in, "So, David, you are saying that Todd and I need to keep our lines of communication open?"

Steve says, "That's right, Sam. And another thing: you need to learn how to deflect praise."

Rebecca has never heard that term used with praise before. "*Deflect* praise?" she asks.

"Yes Rebecca," Steve replies. "One of the devil's favorite techniques is to appeal to our egos. A member seeking power may approach your husband, and say something to the effect that Sam's preaching is better than Todd's, or that Sam is more sensitive than Todd. Or that he or she can talk to Sam more easily than they can to Todd."

Rebecca, usually the serious type, banters with Steve. She says, "And *that* person would be correct!"

Todd misses Rebecca's humor. He agrees with her, "I totally concur."

Rebecca says, "Todd, I was only kidding!" We all laugh.

David speaks. "Rebecca, Sam's response to the power-seeker's disingenuous praise will indicate Sam's level of loyalty to Todd."

I ask, "How is that?"

Steve gives us a scenario. "Let's say, specifically, that a man comes to Todd after he has handled a difficult situation in your church. The man lavishes him with his appreciation. Todd smiles and simply says, 'Thank you.' The man continues, 'I believe that you are one of the greatest leaders I have ever known!'"

I pick up the conversation. "That man would be right. Todd has always been one of the finest leaders at First Church!"

Todd says, "Thanks, Sam."

Steve and David look at each other. The unspoken message: "We probably don't have to worry about any loyalty issues between these two guys." But, to be on the safe side, David interjects, "Todd, the problem arises with your response. When anyone compares you with Sam, or Sam with you, they are basically acting like children. They are trying to pit one of you against the other."

Lisa has been silent for several moments. "What would be the right response to that kind of praise?" she asks.

Steve answers, "To simply *deflect* the praise. Todd could say something to the effect that Sam's superb preaching challenges him to become more committed to Christ and more dependent upon godly wisdom."

"I understand," Todd shouts. "We 'deflect praise' by giving away our praise. I should look for every opportunity to praise Sam, and he should look for every opportunity to praise me!"

Steve continues, once again marveling at the insight of a fellow Saul. "That's very good, Todd! And, once the members realize they cannot turn you against each other they, like the devil in Luke 4:13, will leave you 'until an opportune time.'"

I ask, "You mean he won't come back until he begins to sense disunity between Todd and me?"

"That's right, Sam," Steve replies. "And do you know when that is most likely to happen?"

"I'm not sure, Steve."

"It *will* happen when you hire new staff members. The same disgruntled guy will approach *them* in a similar manner. He will tell him or her that they are somehow a better Bible teacher or a better leader than either you or Todd. If the staff member responds by thanking the person, the power-seeker will continue: 'I believe your teaching abilities are actually *much* better than Sam's,' or 'your solution to that issue was far more impressive than Todd's.' If the staff member thanks the man again, he or she has signaled his or her allegiance to the man, and his or her disloyalty to the two of you."

Rebecca says, "That sounds serious!"

Steve continues, "It is *extremely* serious. Once staff members begin to become puffed up—think too highly of themselves—it is only a matter of time before divisions begin to form in the church. At that point, the best case scenario will be that you will have disunity in the church. The worst case will be that the church will split, and the rebellious staff member will take the helm of the departing group."

David says, "The key to solving the problem is to nip it; nip it in the bud!'[37] And you do that through *instruction* and *observation*. You instruct your staff members as to the proper response to unsolicited praise. You *train* them to deflect any compliments they receive to both you and Sam."

Rebecca, the quintessential Barnabas, is a great listener. She asks, "What about *observation*?"

Steve answers her question. "Observation takes place when any one of the four of you, you ladies are included, notice a staff member becoming a little too friendly with one of the church members." Steve takes it one step further. "In fact, Rebecca, you ladies will often be more observant of interpersonal interactions than will your husbands."

In order to stop another Mutual Admiration Society from forming, I quickly ask, "Is that a problem? Is it wrong for staff

---

[37] A saying coined by Barney Fife, a character portrayed by Don Knotts on the popular television sit-com, "The Andy Griffith Show®."

members to develop close relationships with church members?"

"Not necessarily, Sam," David replies. "But it *could* be. Have you heard of the term, 'compatibility of rebellion'?"

I reply, "I think so. Are you talking about one of Bill Gothard's teachings?"

"Yes, Sam," David continues. "As you probably know, Bill is the founder of the Institute in Basic Life Principles.[38] 'Compatibility of rebellion' is the unseen attraction that one rebellious person will always have for another rebellious person. The old saying, 'Birds of a feather flock together,' is true. A contentious church member will always seek out and, ultimately, find an ally."

"How do we handle that?" Todd asks.

David patiently repeats his earlier statement, "By *education* and *observation*. The four of you will discover and expose, by experience, the church members that are attempting to spread sedition."

David turns his focus upon Todd and me. "Men, you will then watch to see which, if any, of your staff members are becoming too friendly with that person. You should *immediately* take those staff members aside and personally address the issue. You could ask, 'What were you and Fred talking about?' If the staff member

---

[38] http://iblp.org/iblp/, site visited on 6-6-2011.

becomes defensive, you will likely have a problem beginning to form. However, if he or she seems genuinely confused about the question, you may not have a legitimate concern. Either way, you should take the opportunity to inform them of your apprehensions about the particular church member. And you should remind them to constantly develop the habit of deflecting praise to the two pastors."

"*I* can do that," Todd replies.

"I'm not so sure I would be comfortable doing that," I respond.

Steve informs me, "That's why you have Todd. The division of labor in the new church will place the primary responsibility upon the shoulders of the co-pastor best suited for a particular task. And I think we all would agree that Todd will be better suited for handling church conflict."

I say, "Amen to that!" And then I ask, "What about the *unpaid* church leaders, such as the deacons, elders, and teachers? Do we handle them the same way?"

Steve is now impressed with my *Barnabas* insight. "Yes, Sam. You cannot allow *anyone* with any level of authority to become part of a group that will ultimately reject the pastoral leadership of the church."

David returns to the conversation. "I believe this loyalty issue is extremely important. Why don't we break for a few days to surf the net, read articles and books, and meet back on Thursday?"

We all agree. Todd, Lisa, Rebecca and I shake hands with the receiving line that consists of Steve and David. We exit the building together on our way to my favorite restaurant for supper. One thing is for sure: *they* won't be serving leftovers!

Part Two

Thursday arrives. David, Steve, Todd, and I bring our books and articles to the meeting.

David begins, "Are we prepared to have an in-depth discussion regarding loyalty?" We all glance around the room at one another. We nod in agreement.

David continues, "Why don't I start? I have brought one of my all-time favorite books, Stop Setting Goals If You Would Rather Solve Problems.[39] I am not only a Barnabas. I am also a problem solver."

---

[39] Bob Biehl, Stop Setting Goals If You Would Rather Solve Problems, Random House, Inc., 1995.

Steve pretends to be intrigued. He says, "You are a problem *solver*? I thought you were a problem *creator*!"

"That's very funny, Steve," David replies. "You will notice that I am giving you a *courtesy* laugh: ha, ha. No, according to the author, Bob Biehl, there are basically two groups of people: goal setters and problem solvers. I have the God-given ability to see a problem as an opportunity. And I can usually visualize several possible solutions. I then use a mental flowchart to determine the best course of action."

Steve and Todd look at each other. Todd speaks. "That would drive me crazy! I try to avoid problems as much as possible. But, when I *do* encounter one, I attempt to take care of it as quickly as possible."

David replies, "That is because you are a goal setter. You constantly look down the road toward your final destination. Problems, to you, are simply the bumps in the road."

"Hey, that's right!" Todd responds.

Steve adds his thoughts. "And I am also a goal setter. You are describing me, too!"

"I already knew that, Steve," David replies. "And, to make the circle complete, I would imagine that you, Sam, like me, are a problem solver."

I answer, "You have definitely been reading my mail or, possibly, my email. How did you know that?"

"Two reasons, Sam. First, you are a Barnabas. And, in my experience, Barnabases are typically problem solvers. Second, the old saying is true: 'It takes one to know one.'"

Todd, the bottom line guy, says, "So what do these classifications have to do with loyalty?"

I reply, "I believe they would have a great deal to do with it. Obviously, you goal setting Sauls are ready to take an immediate action. On the other hand, we problem solving Barnabases will want to take the time to evaluate the potential results. The difference in timing could definitely become a source of friction between us."

"And not only that, Sam" David says, "the Barnabas and Saul members of the church staff will naturally gravitate toward, and be more loyal to, their pastoral counterparts: Barnabases with Barnabases, and Sauls with Sauls. *Understanding* and *celebrating* these additional classifications of goal setting and problem solving can ensure that the two of you *and* your staff members will get along better together in a long-term ministry."

Steve agrees with David. "I can certainly understand that. You and I (he says, as he points to David) have occasionally disagreed about the 'whens' and the 'hows' of starting some new endeavor."

David quips, laughingly, "*Occasionally?*"

Steve returns, "Well, maybe *frequently* would be a more apt description."

Not surprisingly, Todd becomes impatient. He clears his throat. When he sees that he has our full attention, he says, "I have conducted *my own* research about loyalty."

David recognizes his impatience. He responds, "Why don't you tell us about it?"

"I will," Todd says. He hands us copy of a quote from some guy named Frederick Reichheld. He tells us that Reichheld is "a Director Emeritus of Bain & Company and a Bain Fellow," whatever that means. Todd invites us to read along with him:[40]

> *The six principles of loyalty encompass standards of excellence, simplicity, honesty, fairness, respect, and responsibility. But they are not idealized abstractions far removed from the routine operations of the workaday world. On the contrary, they are embodied in simple, straightforward actions that drive measurement systems, compensation, organization, and strategy:*
>
> *1. Play to win/win – profiting at the expense of partners is a shortcut to a dead end.*

---

[40] Frederick Reichheld, Loyalty Rules: How Today's Leaders Build Lasting Relationship Harvard Press, 2003, pg. 17.

2. *Be picky — membership is a privilege.*
3. *Keep it simple — complexity is the enemy of speed and responsiveness.*
4. *Reward the right results — worthy partners deserve worthy goals.*
5. *Listen hard, talk straight — long-term relationships require honest, two-way communication and learning.*
6. *Preach what you practice — actions often speak louder than words, but together they are unbeatable.*

Since Todd will become my Saul co-pastor, I am compelled to ask the question no one else seems to want to ask. "What does all that mean, Todd?" I am keenly aware, as are the others in the room, that we are about to be served a lengthy lecture. And we will *not* be disappointed.

"It means, Sam, that Reichheld has given us the outline for solving our loyalty issues."

I think, "Todd is a typical goal setter: he believes there is a 'one-size-fits-all,' cookie cutter solution." I ask him to continue. He does. He walks over to the marker board in order to write down the steps. *Even though* the rest of us already have them in print!

"Sam, it's like cleaning a fish: you do it one step at a time. The first step is 'play to win/win.' You remember our situation at First Church? Your opposition had the mentality that they *had* to win at all costs, and that *you* had to lose. Any time one person is willing to sacrifice the needs of other people in order to fulfill his or her agenda, you will have a win/lose situation." He writes "win/win" and "win/lose on the board."

"Next we have, 'be picky — membership is a privilege.'"

"What in the world does *that* mean?" Steve asks.

Todd looks surprised. "Steve, *you* of all people in this room should understand that one! It means that, if you don't *hire* the wrong kinds of people, you won't have to deal with the wrong kinds of *outcomes*. That's where David and Sam will come in. They will use their problem solving skills during the interviewing process to determine the level of loyalty being displayed by each potential employee."

Steve is nonplused. "You mean David and Sam's *intuition*, don't you, Todd? Are you crazy?"

Todd is tenacious. "No, Steve. I have seen Sam successfully demonstrate the power of his *intuition*, as you call it, in several instances over the last few years. And I'm guessing that you have seen David use *his* intuition, also!"

David appears somewhat embarrassed. He says, "Maybe I am a *little* intuitive, but not as much as Sam."

Steve looks disgusted. He says, "I am calling a time out on this 'Mutual Admiration Society.' Todd, can we please move on?"

"Of course we can, Steve. But before we do—we Sauls also bring something to the table."

Steve asks, "What's that, Todd?"

He replies, "We do our homework. We check out the references. We contact the *unnamed* references: the people our candidates *should* have listed on their résumés, but didn't. You and I have demonstrated, time and again, that Jeremiah 13:23 is true."

Steve replies, "You have me on that one. What does Jeremiah say?"

"He says that the leopard cannot change its spots. A candidate with a record of loyalty to his or her previous employer will likely be loyal to a new employer. Conversely, a *disloyal* employee will continue to be disloyal in the future. Loyalty seems to be a trait that you either have it, or you don't. I don't think it can be taught."

David and I marvel at the wisdom flowing from Todd's lips. David looks at me, *jealously*. I think he wishes that he could trade co-pastors with me! I grin, spitefully, back at him.

We are now enrapt by Todd's message. Steve says, "What about number three: keep it simple?"

Partners in Planting

Todd has the ability to jest with a straight face. He says, "That's *simple*, Steve!" We all groan at Todd's attempt at a play on words. He continues, "Read the rest of the quote from Reichheld's third point. He stated that 'complexity is the enemy of speed and responsiveness.' Confusion of our goals will definitely breed disloyalty. You three guys are the Bible scholars. Doesn't it say something about the problems that are associated with a lack of vision?"

David speaks. "It *does*, Todd. The verse is found in Proverbs 29:18: 'Where there is no vision, the people are unrestrained.' Church members will become like a horse that is heading for the barn. And you had better get out of their way!"

"Thank you for making my point, David," Todd replies. He glances my way. "That sounds a little like First Church, doesn't it, Sam?"

I respond, "Yes it does, Todd. In fact, I have another verse. Rather, I have *two* verses that I used for my text toward the end of my tenure there. You may remember them, Todd. Both verses are identical, and are both found in the book of Judges—17:6 and 21:25. 'In those days there was no king in Israel; everyone did what was right in his own eyes.'"

"I *do* remember that sermon, Sam. And, as usual, it was a great one!"

David and Steve exchange glances. The unspoken assertion, "No disloyalty issues between Todd and Sam."

Steve mutters something about another "Mutual Admiration Society."

Todd asks, "I'm sorry. What did you say, Steve?"

"Oh nothing, Todd," he replies.

David interrupts. "I don't know about the rest of you guys, but *I'm* getting hungry! Why don't we go to lunch?" We all agree. He continues, "And, this time, *Steve* is buying!"

Steve agrees, but only after a few moments of *loud* protestation.

Part Three

After we return from lunch, Todd promptly resumes his place at the helm. "Three down, and three more to go. Number four says, 'reward the right results — worthy partners deserve worthy goals.' I practice that at my company as C.F.O. Our new sales manager, Greg Watson, is a Barnabas. *I* set the goals for the sales force. I have given *him* the authority to establish the reward system. He has done a tremendous job! He has developed a strategy for recognizing the producers without discouraging the nonproducers. And some of the n.p.s are beginning to excel! Loyalty is at an all-time high; turnovers are at an all-time low."

Todd continues, "Number five says that we should 'listen hard, talk straight—long-term relationships require honest, two-way communication and learning.' I have heard Zig Ziglar say that people 'don't care how much you know until they know how much you care.' Listening is easy for you Barnabases; Steve and I have to work at it!" Steve nods. "The next part is easy for us Sauls: talking straight. I have found that people would rather know where they really stand than to be told they are doing a great job when, in actuality, they are not. You know, like doctors today. They, unlike the doctors of yesteryear, don't withhold the bad news."

"And now," Todd says, "the point you have all been waiting for—number six. 'Preach what you practice—actions often speak louder than words, but together they are unbeatable.' Since I have only scanned the book, I have no idea what Reichheld meant by this one."

"Maybe I can help," David says. "As a preacher, I have often been told to 'practice what I preach.' Since the author reversed the two, he is putting the emphasis on our *words* over our *actions*. He is saying, 'Say it and *then* live it.' Once people know where you claim to stand on an issue, they will be watching you carefully to determine whether or not you really believe in what you say. So when any one of the four of us issues a pastoral edict, the rest of us had better be prepared to live by it ourselves!"

Todd mulls over David's words. After a moment of ruminating—chewing his cud—he says, "David, I think you are right!"

David smiles as he says, "Of course I'm right, Todd. We Barnabases are *always* right!" David and I laugh quietly; Todd and Steve are hysterical. David continues, "It wasn't *that* funny." The laughter immediately ceases.

Part Four

All eyes are upon *me*. David asks the inevitable question, "Sam, do you have anything that you would like to add to our discussion?"

I respond, "Todd is definitely a hard act to follow. That having been said, I *do* have something to add. I found a book entitled, <u>Why Loyalty Matters</u>. The two authors' names are about as hard to pronounce as some of the names in the Bible, but they have some great thoughts about loyalty. They have formulated an equation called, 'P_2R_2.' Quoting the book, 'P_2R_2 stands for Pinpoint, Prioritize, Reinforce, and Reach Out."[41]

David says, encouragingly, "Sam, tell us what that means."

"That's easy, David. A blogger named Michael McKinney has done all of the work *for* me. He basically took the four points of the authors' equation and expanded upon them in his article entitled, 'Four Steps to Building Loyalty.'[42] He said the first step is to 'pinpoint where you are.' He asks the question, 'Where do you stand?' He continues with the statement, 'We believe we are far more loyal than the recipients of our loyalty believe us to be.'"

Steve asks, "May I expound on that for a moment, Sam?"

I reply, "Certainly, Steve."

Steve continues, "Sam, I believe McKinney is telling us that we tend to deceive ourselves into thinking that we are

---

[41] Timothy Keiningham and Lerzan Aksoy, Why Loyalty Matters: The Groundbreaking Approach to Rediscovering Happiness, Meaning and Lasting Fulfillment in Your Life and Work, BenBella Books: 2010, pg. 207.

[42] http://www.leadershipnow.com/leadingblog/2010/01/four_steps_to_building_loyalty.html, site visited on 6-8- 2011.

demonstrating loyalty when, in fact, we are not. There is a Bible verse that explains this: [43]"

> *For we are not bold to class or compare ourselves with some of those who commend themselves; but when they measure themselves by themselves and compare themselves with themselves, they are without understanding.*

Todd asks, "What does *that* mean, Steve?"

Steve replies, "It means that we all have a tendency to compare our own qualities to the qualities of others in many areas of life — including loyalty. Compared to some people, I may be *extremely* loyal to the organization and the leadership. But I may fall desperately short in that regard in comparison to others. And when I compare myself to Jesus and the loyalty *He* demonstrated to His Father and His Father's plan, I realize I must continue to strive to improve."

"Thank you, Steve," I respond. I wipe the imaginary sweat from my forehead as I say, "Whew, I thought *I* was going to have to explain that one! The next one," I continue, "says":

> *Prioritize those things that matter: if we want to make loyalty a meaningful part of our*

---

[43] 2 Corinthians 10:12.

> *everyday existence, then we need to understand where we are actually spending our time and then prioritize.*

In other words, the blogger is telling us that we can gauge the importance of something in our lives by the amount of time we are willing to invest in it. Since loyalty is crucial to the smooth operation of a church, I would say we need to be *extravagant* in this area. Todd, did you have an opportunity to speak with Mike Jackson about 'Doegs?'"[44]

"I did, Sam. I thought he was saying 'dogs' with a Southern accent!"

"So did I Todd. What did you think about what he said?"

"I thought he was exactly right! We both know a certain staff member at First Church that had a penchant for avoiding work while always managing to find the time he needed to meet with disgruntled church members."

I reply, tongue-in-cheek, "Do you *really* think *so*, Todd? I can't imagine which one of the staff members that could have been."

---

[44] W. Scott Moore, <u>Dead Ends or Destiny: Seven Paths through the Wilderness Experiences of Life</u>. (Rogersville, AL: Eleos Press, 2012), pp. 23-27.

Maintaining the frivolity, Todd says, "Maybe you're right, Sam. I must have only imagined it!"

Steve and David have inquiring minds—they want to know. But Todd and I don't tell.

I continue, "The staff member we are referring to—we won't use his name—avoided meeting with the other staff members like the plague. He even played with his smart phone during our mandatory, weekly staff prayer meetings!"

Steve and Todd exchange glances. Steve speaks. "I don't know about *Todd*, but I would have *snatched* the phone right out of his hand and said, 'We are praying right now. You can have your phone back when we get through!" Todd walks over to Steve, and gives him a "high five."

I continue, "I wish one of you two Sauls would have been there. As a relational Barnabas, I have the tendency to overlook an issue until it becomes too massive to handle."

Todd responds, "It won't happen again. Not when you and I are a team!"

I believe him. "Number three is to, 'reinforce your connections: actively schedule time to connect with those to whom we owe loyalty.' The blogger says, 'It will mean that there will be times we must sacrifice doing things that would be more fun to help a friend in need.' That tells me that 'the road goes both

Partners in Planting

ways.' I cannot expect a staff member to run to my rescue if I have failed to be there for him or her in his or her time of need." As an aside, I mention, "Todd, did you know that I helped our 'Doeg' move into his home?"

"No, I didn't know that, Sam."

I shake my head. "Well, I did. It was cold and rainy, with a mixture of snow. I was on one side of his piano, with his son-in-law on the other!"

David jokes, "Aren't you getting a little old for that sort of thing, Sam?"

I respond, "I know I may look like a wreck now. But, in my day, I was quite the muscle man!"

Steve picks up on the fun, "And what day was that, Sam?"

David piles on. "Guys, let's go easy on Sam. Can't you see that he still has a set of bulging *stomach* muscles?"

"Very funny," I reply. "But you're right, Steve. My 'day' was several years ago, which leads me to point number four (it really doesn't, but I say it anyway): 'reach out to others: engage beyond your friends and family.' McKinney concluded, 'It says, this relationship, this institution, this cause is mine, and I will not abandon it.' In order to develop loyalty in others and myself, I must continually enlarge my circle of influence. I must include every member of the congregation and, if time allows, their unchurched family members and friends. And that certainly includes the people that are serving as our staff members."

David picks up on the thought, "And it is also important to involve *your* family members in the lives of your staff members and their families."

I think, "David must be reading my mail. Rebecca has kept her distance from church members and staff members for years. As a Saul, she has learned to avoid the inevitable controversies. This could become my greatest challenge of all!"

Acceptance

One week later, the four of us—David, Steve, Todd, and I—meet together for our final coaching session.

Steve begins with a question. "Todd and Sam, have you heard about anti-rejection drugs, also known as immunosuppressants?"

I ask, "Immuno *what*?"

Steve continues, "Immunosuppressants. They are drugs that":

> *Help to suppress the immune system's response to a new organ. When a new organ is placed inside a patient's body, the patient's*

> *immune system recognizes the organ as foreign tissue and tries to reject it.*[45]

I reply, "Yes, Steve. Todd and I have both heard of them." I look at Todd as I say, "Haven't we, Todd?" Todd nods his head in agreement.

Steve asks, "Would you both agree, then, that the most foreign object to a Barnabas is a Saul, and vice versa?" We both vigorously signal our agreement.

David says, "I am sure that the two of you also understand that you will have a natural tendency to reject each other?"

In unison, Todd and I reply, "Yes."

Todd asks, "So, what is the solution? What will we use for an immunosuppressant?"

Steve enjoys the no-nonsense approach of his fellow Saul. He says, "Todd, the best *drug* we can administer to the two of you will be prayer. The old saying, 'the family that prays together stays together' may sound trite. But it works! We recommend that the two of you, along with your wives, spend at least one hour a week together in prayer."

Todd, forming a mental checklist, says, "Okay. What else?"

---

[45] http://medical-dictionary.thefreedictionary.com/Anti-Rejection+Drugs, site visited on 2-2-2012.

David says, "You should also spend some recreational time together. According to Belton S. Wall, Jr.: Homer Lindsay, Jr. and Jerry Vines 'became fast friends, and on occasion the two families vacationed together.'"[46]

I protest, and loudly. "Surely you aren't suggesting that we should share our vacation times? Haven't you guys heard about the secret to getting along?" The three men shake their heads. I continue, "A man said that he and his wife had been married for fifty years. He said that their 'secret' was taking two weeks of vacation every year. He concluded, 'She takes *her* vacation one week, I take *mine* on another.'"

Three men consolidate their energies to give me one courtesy laugh. David continues, "No, Sam, we are not recommending that you and Todd take a combined family vacation. You *will* need some time alone with your wives and children."

Steve says, "But what we *are* suggesting is that you spend time together apart from your responsibilities at the church. Every couple of months, David and I take our wives out together for dinner and a movie."

David proposes, "And we also take all of our kids to the park for a picnic during the summer."

---

[46] Wall, <u>A Tale to be Told</u>, p. 71.

Partners in Planting

Todd responds, "Okay, Sam and I get the picture. Is there anything else?"

Steve says, "Yes, Todd. There is one other thing. You will both need accountability partners."

I ask, "I thought *Todd* was my accountability partner, and that *I* was his?"

David answers, "Yes Sam, in a sense that is true. But you will each need accountability partners *beyond* yourselves."

Todd asks, "And who might that be?"

Steve replies, "David and I. *We* will be your accountability partners."

"How will that work?" I ask.

Steve concludes, "We will alternate. You, Sam, will meet with me once every even-numbered month to elicit *my* feedback in better understanding Todd." He turns to Todd as he says, "And you, Todd, will meet with David once every even-numbered month to elicit *his* feedback in better understanding Sam."

Not content to leave well enough alone, I ask, "What about the odd-numbered months?"

David smiles at Steve. He says, "I think we just caught another fish!" He looks at me as he says, "On the odd-numbered months, you will meet with me."

Steve looks at Todd. "And, Todd, you will meet with me."

Todd says, "I think I understand. That way we can utilize our counterparts to commiserate—to sympathize—with us for having to work with our 'foreign tissue.'"

I interrupt, "Hey, Todd, I resemble that remark." Three sets of eyes roll and three heads move together in affirmation. I think, "*Finally, we are all in agreement.*"

The Ministry Team

The four of us—David, Steve, Todd, and I—meet together one week later. Today's agenda is to select our ministry team.

David explains, "Todd and Sam, you will need several team members. We will give you a list of fifteen men and women—all *loyal* members of New Wine Church—that are ready to work with you in starting the new church."

"Fifteen!" I shout. "That's enough for a small church plant!"

David looks pained. "No, Sam, you and Todd can't have *all* of them. You will have to pick *five*."

I am puzzled. "We can only have five of them? How will we know which ones to pick?"

Steve speaks. "We will help you with that, Sam."

Todd asks, "David, you mentioned that all of the applicants have been prescreened with regard to their levels of loyalty to the leadership of New Wine Church?"

David answers, "That is correct, Todd. We would never recommend potential staff members, no matter how qualified they may be, unless they have been able to pass the crucible of loyalty."

"I am certainly glad to hear that," I respond.

David continues, "Let me explain the selection process. We will begin the process with 15 applicants. We will narrow the pool of 15 candidates down to the top ten, using the Ministry Insights® Assessment.[47] The website makes the following claims":

- *See your God-given strengths in detail*
- *Increase personal and mutual understanding*
- *Decrease interpersonal conflict among team members*
- *Learn how others are motivated*
- *Increase productivity with accurate expectations*
- *Assess how your strengths complement those closest to you*

---

[47] http://www.lifeway.com/article/167760/, site visited on 6-2-2011.

- *Assess and compare how you best communicate with others*
- *Learn the best ways to blend your differences with others*
- *Uncover the ideal ministry environment for your most effective service*

Steve continues the explanation. "Sam, do you remember that website you and I have both used in evaluating couples during premarital counseling?"

"Yes, Steve. Prepare-Enrich™,"[48] I reply.

"We can adapt the program by simply pretending that Todd is *marrying* all ten of the remaining applicants." He says, parenthetically, "I guess that means you and Todd is now a *Mormon*." Steve and David laugh.

I have an "ah ha" moment. "I see, Steve. So we will use this process to bypass a lot of relational issues that could later become serious problems in the early stages of establishing the new church?"

---

[48] https://www.prepare-enrich.com/webapp/pe/overview/template/DisplaySecureContent.vm;pc=1328621892906;jsessionid=47ABD363FB73416658DF7E3C7FD0487A?id=pe*prepare_enrich*introduction.html&emb_org_id=0&emb_sch_id=0&emb_lng_code=ENGLISH, site visited on 2-7-2012.

Partners in Planting

"That's right, Sam!" David exclaims. He looks at Steve. "See, Steve, I told you Sam is the right man for the job."

"I knew it all along, David," Steve responds. "Don't forget—*I* was the one that called *you*! I told you that Sam was our guy."

David concedes, "I know, Steve. I know."

David turns his attention back to me. "Sam, as I said, you and Todd will select the five members of your team. We have a rule at New Wine: the person, or *group*, with the authority to hire and fire staff members is the person, or group, that supervises them. For the record, I *personally* supervise the New Wine staff. Do you catch my drift?"

Scratching my chin I say, "So you are telling me that Todd and I will have the power to hire and fire the members of our team?"

David answers, "Yes, Sam, but *Todd* will have the primary responsibility and authority in that area. Based upon our discussion of the division of labor, Barnabases are better suited for hiring the employees, and Sauls are better suited for firing the employees"

"I do, David. So Todd will be primarily responsible for employee terminations?"

David continues, "Yes, Sam. And, right up front, you and Todd will need to apprise everyone on your team of that fact. We hope and pray that neither one of you ever has to exercise that authority, but you will have it, nonetheless. You will soon discover that every policy we have established at New Wine Church has been based upon the clear teachings we have gleaned from the Bible. This particular principle has been taken from Matthew 6:24: 'No one can serve two masters.' We have found that staff members will function best when they have only one person to whom they will be required to answer. In your case, they will report *exclusively* to Todd."

Without thinking, I revert to my high school days. I raise my hand. David says, "Put your hand down, Sam. Do you have a question?"

"Yes, David," I reply. "All of that makes sense. But what about the church members, will *they* have input in leading the staff?"

Steve answers, "No, Sam, they won't. Your staff members will receive all of their instructions directly from Todd."

Todd adds, "Sam, that arrangement will alleviate a great deal of frustration for our staff members. They won't be pulled in several different directions as they attempt to cater to the whims of the entire congregation."

David says, "That's right, Todd. And this arrangement has also gone a long way in both building and maintaining staff member loyalty at New Wine. And it will at your new church, also."

I nod my head enthusiastically. I think, "I wish I had known about this at First Church. That would certainly have made a difference!"

I ask, "So when does Todd take the surveys with our staff candidates?"

Steve responds, "I have good news and bad news. The good news is that David and I have already used the Ministry Insights® Assessment to narrow the field to ten. And, additionally, all ten of the remaining applicants have already completed their parts of the Prepare-Enrich™ evaluation."

I ask, "So, what's the bad news?"

Steve replies, "The bad news is that Todd will have to go online and take the test ten separate times using ten fictitious names!"

Todd hears us using his name. He immediately rejoins the conversation. "You must be kidding, Steve!"

"I am, Todd. We have nine volunteers that will help to key in your responses. We will use the 'Flying V' method perfected by one of the fraternities at my college."

Todd asks, "Steve, what in the world is a 'Flying V?'"

The "Flying V"

"It was a means of improving fraternity members' test scores. The fraternity members would invite one 'nerd' to join their ranks for the purpose of helping the others in taking their tests. The nerd would sit in the front of the lecture hall during an exam. Two of the fraternity brothers would sit one row behind him, one to his right and the other to his left (see the diagram above). The two would look at the nerd's test paper and copy his answers. Two more fraternity brothers would sit behind the brothers on the second row, one to the left side of the left brother and one to the right side of the right brother. The 'V' could continue, theoretically, all the way to the back of the room."

I shout, "That's terrible Steve!" I warily ask, "Did *you* do that?"

Steve responds, "I cannot tell a lie. *I* was the nerd in the front of the room!"

David can't resist. "Steve, you're still a nerd!" We all laugh.

"So anyway, Todd," Steve continues, "you can sit in the front of the room with your desktop computer. Two of the volunteers can sit behind you, one on your left side and one on your right side. You, accompanied by the four double rows and one single row of volunteers, will punch in the answers. And, voila, we will have our 'Flying V!'"

David regains control. He says, "Todd, the purpose of all this will be that, in one sitting, we can determine your compatibility with all ten of the remaining applicants. We will receive immediate feedback from the website, pick our five finalists, and make appointments for you and Sam to meet with each one individually. If, for some reason, either one of you is uncomfortable with one of the applicants, we will invite applicant number six to come in for an interview."

Not to be left out, I chime in, "That sounds like the process for striking a jury."

David concludes, "That's right, Sam. Except for the fact that some of these 'jurors' will be working with you and Todd for many years to come."

Start Date

Todd and I meet together without David and Steve. We have been charged with one primary responsibility: to determine the launch date of the new church.

"Todd," I begin, "we have been training with David and Steve for three months. They are recommending we take several months for team member training. When do you think we should hold our 'grand opening'? In other words, what day would you suggest for our launch date?"

"You know me, Sam—the sooner the better!"

"I understand that, Todd. But, as a problem solving Barnabas, I don't think we need to rush the process."

Todd continues, "We could throw out an arbitrary date, say six months from today, and work our way back using a step-by-step preparation process."

I respond, "Since we are going with arbitrary dates, Todd, why don't we make it nine months from today? Added to the three months of training we have just completed, we would then have completed a full *year* of preparation."

"Okay, Sam. Nine more months it is."

"So, Todd, if I understand David and Steve correctly, they are going to help us with the resources we will need for the launch." Todd nods in agreement. "*They* have *already* provided us with the five members of our new ministry team, including our worship leader, our singers and musicians, our nursery coordinator, and our Bible teachers."

Todd interjects, "And, don't forget, we also have our wives."

"That's right, Todd," I say jokingly, "I almost forgot! And the members of New Wine Church will also provide us with the advertisement for our new start. Their church members will mail out letters to everyone in our neighborhood, place phone calls letting people know about the new church, place the newspaper ads, and make door-to-door visits."

"That *is* incredible, isn't it, Sam?"

"It surely is, Todd. I have heard stories of mission pastors that have spent several years trying to build a church. They start with a handful of people and, with a lot of hard work, end up years later with only 100 people. On the other hand, churches that plan ahead and start with a launch date will almost immediately have 100 people *or more!*"

Todd says, "It almost seems unfair, doesn't it?"

"Not to me, Todd. We Barnabas problem solvers are always looking for more efficient ways of doing things."

Todd knows the true meaning of my statement. "Don't you mean the *easiest* way of doing things?"

I reply, "Most efficient. Easiest. To me, they are synonymous."

Todd smiles as he mentally begins his process of planning. "Okay, Sam," he says. "Let's not waste the entire nine months just sitting here daydreaming. With regard to the ministry team, I think we need to meet with them at least once a week for the entire nine months."

"I agree, Todd. But remember: we have been instructed to continue attending the worship services of the various churches that we have already been attending each week. The training times would be *in addition to* our worship time, not as substitutions *for* them."

"I understand that, Sam. Since we are only attending church services on Sunday mornings, why don't we meet together on Sunday nights?"

"That makes sense, Todd."

"Thank you, Sam. I still think we can accomplish all of our preparation in six months. Why do you think it will take nine?"

Partners in Planting

"Well let's see, Todd. Even though you have already completed the team member *testing*, our joint *interviewing* process will still take several more weeks. As I have already mentioned, team member *training* will take a minimum of three months. That's a total, so far, of four months. Lee Thompson and the members of Riverside Church have begun construction of our first building. That will, of course, overlap with everything else we have discussed. I spoke with the contractor last week. He said that it will take about six more months to complete."

"See, I'm right," Todd says. "Six months!"

I pull my trump card. "And will the new building be fully furnished upon completion?" Todd looks quietly at me. "And will the parking lot be paved upon completion of the building?" I answer my own question, "I don't think so! That will take another couple of weeks."

I am now piling on. "And do you think we might want to have a few practice runs in the new building with the worship team before we invite our first crowd to a public worship service? And what about the inevitable glitches that will happen with the sound system? And don't forget about the lighting."

"Okay, Sam, you win! We will set the date for nine months from today."

Since I have the upper hand, I ask, "And will nine months from today be a Sunday?"

"You know what I mean, Sam! Do you want to have our first disagreement?"

"Our *first* disagreement," I reply. "Have you forgotten the time…"

Without waiting for the details, he replies, "No, Sam, I haven't." He shakes his head as he continues, "You, Lisa, and my sales manager, Greg, are like three peas in a pod! You Barnabases will be the death of me!"

I smile. "But remember, Todd—when you die you get to go to Heaven!"

Todd breathes a sigh of exasperation. He replies, "Your jokes are as corny as the state of Nebraska!"

"I *like* corn, Todd."

With a resigned look, Todd slowly agrees, "So do I, Sam. So do I."

Appendix: A Composite Model

Many growing churches have adopted two basic leadership models. The first, an assembly line approach to ministry, offers several benefits to a church. The method has, correspondingly, many offsetting limitations.

A second model is the team ministry approach. This method also has several strengths and counteracting weaknesses.

An alternative to both leadership models is a composite approach to ministry. This option is a blending of the best elements of both the assembly line and group ministry approaches.

Assembly Line Approach

Definition and Description

The assembly line is identified as an "industrial arrangement of machines, equipment, and workers for continuous flow of workpieces in mass-production operations."[49] It is further characterized as an "arrangement whereby the work in process passes progressively from one operation to the next until the product is assembled."[50]

A Process

An assembly line approach to ministry is, therefore, the process of taking a new believer

---

[49] "Assembly line." Encyclopædia Britannica. Encyclopædia Britannica Multimedia Edition. Chicago: Encyclopædia Britannica, 2011.
[50] Microsoft Encarta Encyclopedia, 1999 ed., s.v. "Assembly Line."

Partners in Planting

through a series of spiritual growth steps. Members achieve the "finished product" status when they reach the goal of spiritual maturity.

The first step in the typical assembly line process is to bring together the "raw materials" by locating lost people and leading them to faith in Jesus Christ. Soul-winning is certainly essential to the life of every church. Growing assembly line churches often perform this function remarkably well.

Second, the new converts are presented publicly to the church. They are usually allowed to receive baptism at the next service. They commonly receive little or no instruction regarding either the meaning or the procedure of baptism.

The newly baptized converts are granted full status as church members. They immediately acquire all associated privileges, including the right to vote in church business meetings.

Next, the recent believers are assigned to one or more sub-groupings within the church. They are encouraged to attend age-graded classes to study the Bible. These classes are designed to serve as the infrastructures for meeting the new converts' needs for both small group Bible study and Christian fellowship.

Fourth, at some point the new converts are usually offered opportunities to become involved in ministry. These believers are frequently viewed as having completed the growth process once they have reached this level of spiritual involvement.

Associated Style of Leadership

Church leaders generally fall into one of two main leadership categories: those that are task-oriented and those that are people-oriented. Task-oriented leaders "place . . . doing ahead of being."[51] Conversely, people-oriented leaders tend to "put . . . being ahead of doing."[52]

The former, task-orientation, is the style of leadership often associated with the assembly line model. Church leaders that adopt this approach are usually more concerned with immediate, quantifiable results (baptisms, attendance, and offerings) than with the Christian growth and development of the current membership.

---

[51] C. Peter Wagner, <u>Leading Your Church to Growth: The Secret of Pastor/People Partnership in Dynamic Church Growth</u> (Ventura, CA: Regal Books, 1984), 100.

[52] Ibid., 100.

Benefits of Task-Orientation

The results-orientation style of leadership associated with an assembly line approach to ministry has one distinct benefit: the small investment necessary per convert. This benefit can be manifested in the church in several ways.

Minimal Time Investment

The first resource conservation is related to the industrial application of the assembly line--the speed of production. Many units can be assembled in a relatively short period of time.

Similarly, many new converts can be "processed" by the church in a brief interval of time. This feature is particularly helpful as a church experiences a period of rapid growth.

This concept was demonstrated through the philosophy of industrialist Henry Ford. L. Scott Bailey, publisher and president of Automobile Quarterly, stated: "Henry Ford pioneered in improving assembly line methods to cut production costs. . . . The big saving of time (emphasis added) cut Ford's production costs."[53] The discipleship process of the individual is, therefore, usually very brief.

Minimal Financial Obligation

The investment per unit is also necessarily lower due to the economic law of supply and demand. Increased production costs will result in a correspondingly higher price per unit. Higher prices subsequently bring about a reduction in consumer demand. Price per unit, therefore, must be kept to a minimum to maintain the company's market position.

The investment per new convert is similarly limited. It must be confined to a percentage of the total number of assigned resources. The financial and personnel constraints of the church are necessarily reflected in the amounts that are available to be allocated to the individual believers.

---

[53] World Book Encyclopedia, 1985 ed., s.v. "Automobile."

Minimal Innovation Expense

The required investment per convert is also reduced because, with new Christians, there is little need for innovation. The same teachers and teaching materials can be used interchangeably with each new group of believers. Churches employing the assembly line method, consequently, Bailey validated the rationale behind this assertion by stating:

> *Basic changes in the body, engine, suspension, or transmission would be too costly to make every year. The yearly changes usually involve such relatively minor improvements as restyled fenders, radiator grilles, or tail lights.*[54]

Church leaders have discovered that they need only make minor modifications to the available resources without sacrificing the quality of personnel and materials available to their constituency.

---

[54] Ibid.

Limitations

The assembly line approach has several inherent limitations. These deficiencies include the impersonal nature of the method, an underutilization of personnel, and an inadequate assimilation of new members.

Impersonal Nature

The first limitation is the impersonal nature of an assembly line approach. The new convert trusts Jesus through the witness of one member of the church. The ministry of the familiar church member often concludes when the new convert joins the church. Depending upon the size of the church, the two people may rarely interact.

The new convert is automatically enrolled into an existing Sunday school class. Sole responsibility for the new believer is thereby transferred to the teacher. The problem is compounded because, generally, the most effective teachers have growing classes. They are thereby limited in effectively working with their class members on an individual basis.

The more established a class becomes the greater the probability it will be composed of closed cliques within the current membership. The members of these inner circles will either see little need or have little desire to welcome the new converts.

Class leaders may attempt to remedy the situation by occasionally hosting some type of fellowship function.

These functions may have a moderate degree of success in welcoming a few of the new members into the class. They are, however, usually ineffective in making any permanent changes.

Church attendance does not guarantee that new converts will be accepted into a group. Conversations before the service are frequently discouraged, as members are expected to enter a time of personal and corporate worship.

The current members will often meet for a few moments after the service. They will discuss common areas of interest. The new members do not share the same frame of reference; they are, once again, excluded from fellowship with the group.

Inefficient Use of People Resources

A second limitation associated with the assembly line is the inefficient use of the appropriation of people resources. John G.

Truxal, with reference to the automotive industry, asserted: "Many people find repetitive, simple jobs, such as working on a factory assembly line, dull and degrading."[55] He further stated: "They have difficulty maintaining the level of interest necessary to do this type of work effectively over long periods of time."[56] Henry Ford also found this circumstance to be true in his experience with the assembly line:[57]

> *By early 1914 this innovation, although greatly increasing productivity, had resulted in a monthly labor turnover of 40 to 60 percent in his factory, largely because of the unpleasant monotony of assembly line work and repeated increases in the production quotas assigned to the workers.*

Ambitious, successful people do not find assembly line ministries very rewarding. These people thrive on ministerial challenges. Few

---

[55] World Book Encyclopedia, 1985 ed., s.v. "Automation."

[56] Ibid., 917.

[57] Funk and Wagnall's Encyclopedia, 1998 ed., s.v. "Henry Ford."

opportunities for meaningful service are offered through the assembly line approach to ministry.

Quality volunteers in an organization also expect recognition for a job well done. Little credit is given to those ministering productively in an assembly line environment.

Inadequate Assimilation

A third limitation may be attributed to the fact that little or no instruction is given to aid in their assimilation into the Christian community.

Team Ministry

A recent innovation for many churches is the "team ministry" concept. This model of church leadership also has several benefits. The model also has some offsetting limitations.

Definition and Description

A team may be defined as: "a number of persons associated together in work or activity."[58] A team ministry model, accordingly, is a group of Christians that share the ministry responsibilities of a local church.

The team ministry approach is a simple two-step process: selection of the team members and involvement in ministry. Prospects for team membership are generally limited to the current constituency of the church. Qualities such as spiritual gifts and Christian maturity help determine members' potential for productive ministries.

Second, the team members are involved in ministry. Training is involved in this step to help fulfill assigned responsibilities. This can be accomplished both through observation of the current members of a team and by means of personal involvement.

Associated Style of Leadership

People-orientation is the style of leadership commonly found in team ministry

---

[58] <u>Merriam Webster's Collegiate Dictionary, 10th Edition</u>
(Springfield, MA: Merriam-Webster, Inc., 1995), 1209.

churches. Leaders exercising this style recognize an important fact: "people must not be treated as simply means toward an end--the end or the goals must be established according to the needs of the people."[59]

Benefits

A people-oriented team ministry is based on the observation that the members of an organization are significant. This rationale has several resultant advantages.

Commitment to Quality

One major advantage of the team approach is an increased commitment to quality. The individual members of the group hold each other accountable for their contributions to the overall ministry process.

Quality is also ensured by the increased likelihood of team member innovation. James B. Miller, founder and Chief Executive Officer of Miller Business Systems, stated: "Employees can

---

[59] Wagner, Leading Your Church to Growth, 100.

provide the fresh perspective and creativity they gain from interacting with customers every day."[60]

Promotion of Spiritual Growth

A second benefit of the team ministry is that it promotes the spiritual growth of church members. According to research specialist Charles Barna: "Unless the church challenge[s] the individual to develop his or her abilities, chances [are] good that the individual [will] not grow."[61] These leadership abilities can readily be nurtured and developed in an environment of shared ministerial responsibilities.

---

[60] James B. Miller, The Corporate Coach (New York: St. Martin's Press, 1993), 82.

[61] Charles Barna, User Friendly Churches: What Christians Need to Know About the Churches People Love to Go To (Ventura, CA: Regal Books, 1991), 166.

Endurance over Time

A third benefit of the team ministry model is that the ministry has the ability to survive beyond the tenure of the current leadership group. John Maxwell is a former pastor, a motivational speaker, and the founder of INJOY Ministries. He asserted: "True success comes only when every generation continues to develop the next generation."[62]

Facilitation of Relationships

A fourth benefit of the team ministry is the facilitation of interpersonal relationships within the church. These associations may facilitate the numerical growth of the congregation. According to Peter Wagner and John L. Gorsuch: "Growing churches put a

---

[62] John Maxwell, <u>Developing the Leaders Around You: How To Help Others Reach Their Full Potential</u> (Nashville: Thomas Nelson Publishers, 1995), 198.

higher priority on this [fellowship] than nongrowing churches."[63]

Limitations

A team ministry also has several inherent limitations. These limitations include the amount of time required for proper implementation of the ministry, the possibility of missed witnessing opportunities, and the increased potential for power struggles within the leadership core.

Time Factor

The first limitation of the team approach is the amount of time invested in the team building process. A leader's personal resources

---

[63] C. Peter Wagner and Richard L. Gorsuch, "The Quality Church (Part 1)," Leadership Winter 1983, 31, quoted in John N. Vaughan, The Large Church: A Twentieth-Century Expression of the First-Century Church (Grand Rapids: Baker Book House, 1985), 99.

must be devoted to equipping church members to function as a team.

John Maxwell alleged: "Equipping, like nurturing, is an ongoing process. You don't equip a person in a few hours or a day. . . . Equipping must be tailored to each potential leader."[64]

Missed Opportunities

A second limitation is in the potential loss of soul-winning opportunities. The exclusive use of a team ministry method can interfere with church leaders' resources of time and energy. Leaders must demonstrate flexibility in their scheduling to meet prospects from the lost community and properly cultivate those relationships.

Potential for Power Struggles

A team ministry approach presents a greater potential for power struggles among the church leaders. One reason for the increased

---

[64] Maxwell, Developing the Leaders Around You, 84.

capacity for disagreement is the method is not conducive to the development of a centralized power structure. A single, autocratic leader is not required to either recognize or consider the opinions of others.

Another reason for the increased potential for leader disagreement is related to the first: team ministries generally create a broader base of control. The propensity for conflict within the group is proportionate to the number of trained leaders in the local church.

A Composite Ministry

The implementation of a composite approach to ministry is a two-step process. The first step is to consider the five basic ministry purposes for the church. The subsequent step is to match each of the five purposes to the most appropriate ministry types for fulfillment.

Five Basic Ministry Purposes

Rick Warren, Senior Pastor of the Saddleback Valley Community Church in

Orange County, California, has identified five basic purposes for the church. The descriptive words for these purposes are: magnify, mission, membership, maturity, and ministry.

Magnify

The first word, magnify, describes the purpose of "celebrat[ing] God's presence in worship."[65] All believers have the responsibility of worshiping God on a regular basis. They must practice this activity both corporately in the local church and individually on a more personal basis.

Mission

Mission, as used by Warren, is "communicat[ing] God's Word through evangelism."[66] Leaders must incorporate the

---

[65] Rick Warren, The Purpose Driven Church: Growth Without Compromising Your Message and Mission (Grand Rapids: Zondervan Publishing House, 1995), 107.
[66] Warren, The Purpose Driven Church, 107.

element of evangelism if they want their churches to reach people and grow numerically.

Membership

The third descriptive word to describe the purpose of the church is membership. Membership is defined as the "incorporat[ion of] God's family into . . . [the] fellowship . . . [of a church]."[67]

Maturity

Maturity is "educat[ing] God's people through discipleship."[68] Churches should be the primary agents for assisting believers in spiritual growth.

---

[67] Ibid., 107.

[68] Ibid., 107.

Ministry

Rick Warren stated that the church has the responsibility to "demonstrate God's love through service."[69] All believers are called to perform some facet of a personal ministry as representatives of the local church.

Most Appropriate Ministry Types

The assembly line method, based upon its unique strengths, is the best choice for fulfilling the purposes of evangelism and assimilation of members. Conversely, utilization of the team ministry approach is more advantageous in fulfilling the purposes of worship, discipleship, and Christian service.

Evangelism and Assimilation

The assembly line model is especially suited for handling the entry stages of church

---

[69] Ibid., 107.

membership. These stages include the purposes of "mission" (evangelism) and "membership" (assimilation).

First, the evangelistic efforts of a church can be managed through an assembly line approach. The process of conversion is one that does not require constant revision.

Most church members can be trained in soul-winning methodologies. They can distribute and explain gospel tracts with prospects. These members are also capable of learning and sharing a simple plan of salvation (such as the "Romans Road").

Second, follow-up of converts ("assimilation") can be handled successfully through the assembly line method. All new believers can be given an identical explanation of the need for baptism and church membership.

The assembly line method can also accommodate new believers' classes. The basic tenets of the Christian life can be explained by means of an ongoing class structure. The assembly line is also useful in acclimating new church members. A standard class can be formed to explain the unique belief structures and characteristics of the church.

Worship, Discipleship, and Christian Service

The team ministry model is especially appropriate for dealing with the three developmental stages of church membership. First, a ministry team could be constructed to assist in the purpose of worship ("magnify"). Second, a ministry team can more effectively handle the discipleship ("maturity") aspects of the church. Third, a ministry team could be assigned the service ("ministry") functions of the congregation.

The members of a worship team could coordinate the efforts of several segments within the local church to produce a more effective overall ministry that honors the Lord. One segment of the worship team could focus on the overall atmosphere of the church during the various services throughout the week. They could assist in such factors as preliminary prayer, planning the orders of service, and decoration of the sanctuary.

Another segment of the worship team could focus on age-graded choirs. A subgroup working with the children's choirs would consist of several members that recognize the importance of teaching children to worship the

Lord at an early age. Those that assist the teenagers might focus on instructing them in a greater understanding of the concept of properly praising the Lord. Another segment would be responsible for working with the adult choirs.

Additional workers could prepare for each service through prayer. They could also establish teams to pray for peoples' needs during the services.

A team can competently facilitate the spiritual growth of church members. The team approach can be used successfully for at least two fundamental reasons: a smaller teacher-disciple ratio and greater accountability.

First, a smaller teacher-disciple ratio allows for more personal time with each convert. This arrangement can be beneficial to both the disciples and the teachers.

The disciples benefit from the exchange because they are personally challenged to follow through with the discipleship exercises. They also have more latitude in interaction with their teachers—obtaining answers that will assist them in understanding the concepts presented. Additionally, disciples in small group situations are more likely allowed the privilege of observing their teachers' responses to real-life situations.

The teachers also profit from the arrangement. Jesus stated a principle in Mark 8:35 (KJV): "For whosoever will save his life shall lose it; but whosoever shall lose his life for my sake and the gospel's, the same shall save it." Counselor Les Carter and businessman Jim Underwood likewise observed: "people can find their own significance by actively touching the lives of others."[70]

The assignment of discipleship responsibilities to a team automatically increases the obligation of the members. Each can hold the others accountable for such items as curriculum selection, lesson preparation, and group member follow-up.

Service

Third, a ministry team would be the proper choice to perform and coordinate the service responsibilities assigned to the church. A team is needed to perform ministry functions because of the direction given by the Apostle

---

[70] Les Carter and Jim Underwood, The Significance Principle: The Secret Behind High Performance People and Organizations (Nashville: Broadman and Holman Publishers, 1998), 198.

Paul in 1 Corinthians 12:4-7 (KJV):

> *Now there are varieties of gifts, but the same Spirit. And there are varieties of ministries, and the same Lord. There are varieties of effects, but the same God who works all things in all persons. But to each one is given the manifestation of the Spirit for the common good.*

A team can also be helpful in establishing a suitable framework for ministry. Team members can work together in certain ministries, assist one another in accountability needs, and form a council to provide the necessary leadership to properly carry out each ministry

CONCLUSION

Most churches have consciously, or unconsciously, adopted either the assembly line method or the team ministry approach. A church can effectively minister using either program.

The most effective churches will first pray for guidance. They will then select the best possible combination of the two.

A composite ministry method can be infinitely variable. The leadership of the church can best determine the purposes that should be fulfilled through the assembly line or as a team. Individual purposes can also be accomplished through a mixture of the two.

The greatest need, therefore, is to examine the church and make the choice. Traditional patterns cannot be perpetuated simply because they are uncomplicated.

The church is obligated to perform a ministry at its highest possible level. The composite ministry is one of many tools that can assist in reaching this primary goal.

BIBLIOGRAPHY

"Assembly line." Encyclopædia Britannica. <u>Encyclopædia Britannica Multimedia Edition</u>. Chicago: Encyclopædia Britannica, 2011.

Barna, Charles. <u>User Friendly Churches: What Christians Need to Know About the Churches People Love to Go To</u> (Ventura, CA: Regal Books, 1991), 166.

Biehl, Bob. <u>Stop Setting Goals If You Would Rather Solve Problems</u>, (Random House, Inc., 1995).

Carter, Les and Jim Underwood. <u>The Significance Principle: The Secret Behind High Performance People and Organizations</u> (Nashville: Broadman and Holman Publishers, 1998).

Dogs of C-Kennel, © 2010 Mick Mastroianni, all rights reserved.

<u>Funk and Wagnall's Encyclopedia</u>, 1998 ed., s.v. "Henry Ford."

http://gregatkinson.com/?s=%22no+vision%22, site visited on 6-1-2011.

http://iblp.org/iblp/, site visited on 6-6-2011.

http://medical-dictionary.thefreedictionary.com/Anti-Rejection+Drugs, site visited on 2-2-2012.

http://smartleadersnetwork.com/2011/01/12/lessons-learned-from-john-maxwell-part-2/, "Let Your Leaders Fly for a While," site visited on 6-5-2011.

http://wiki.answers.com/Q/Where_did_the_expression_%27It_ain%27t_over_til%27_the_fat_lady_sings%27_originate, site visited on 6-7-2011.

http://www.fbcjax.com/about,site visited on 2-1 1-2012.

http://www.leadershipnow.com/leadingblog/2010/01/four_steps_to_building_loyalty.html, site visited on 6-8-2011.

http://www.lifeway.com/article/167760/, site visited on6-2-2011.

http://www.thedisciplemakers.com/?cat=11, site visited on 6-1-2011.

https://www.prepare-
	enrich.com/webapp/pe/overview/templ
	ate/DisplaySecureContent.vm;pc=132862
	1892906;jsessionid=47ABD363FB73416658
	DF7E3C7FD0487A?id=pe*prepare_enrich
	*introduction.html&emb_org_id=0&emb_
	sch_id=0&emb_lng_code=ENGLISH, site
	visited on 2-7-2012.

Keiningham, Timothy and Lerzan Aksoy. Why
	Loyalty Matters: The Groundbreaking
	Approach to Rediscovering Happiness,
	Meaning and Lasting Fulfillment in Your
	Life and Work, (BenBella Books: 2010).

Maxwell, John. Developing the Leaders Around
	You: How To Help Others Reach Their
	Full Potential (Nashville: Thomas Nelson
	Publishers, 1995).

MERRIAM-WEBSTER'S COLLEGIATE
	DICTIONARY AND THESAURUS,
	DELUXE AUDIO EDITION®, Version
	2.5, Copyright © Merriam-Webster,
	Incorporated, 47 Federal Street, P.O. Box
	28l, Springfield, MA 01102.

Microsoft Encarta Encyclopedia, 1999 ed., s.v.
	"Assembly Line."

Miller, James B. The Corporate Coach (New York: St. Martin's Press, 1993).

Moore, W. Scott. Dead Ends or Destiny: Seven Paths through the Wilderness Experiences of Life. (Rogersville, AL: Eleos Press, 2012).

Reichheld, Frederick. Loyalty Rules: How Today's Leaders Build Lasting Relationship (Harvard Press, 2003).

Stack, Debi. Martha to the Max: Balanced Living for Perfectionists, (Chicago: Moody Press, 2000).

Tan, Paul Lee, *Encyclopedia of 7,700 Illustrations*, (Garland, Texas: Bible Communications, Inc., 1996).

Wagner, C. Peter and Richard L. Gorsuch. "The Quality Church (Part 1)," Leadership Winter 1983, 31, quoted in John N. Vaughan, The Large Church: A Twentieth-Century Expression of the First-Century Church (Grand Rapids: Baker Book House, 1985).

Wagner, C. Peter. <u>Leading Your Church to Growth: The Secret of Pastor/People Partnership in Dynamic Church Growth</u> (Ventura, CA: Regal Books, 1984).

Wall, Belton S. <u>A Tale to be Told: the History of the First Baptist Church of Downtown, Jacksonville</u>. (Jacksonville, FL: First Baptist, Jacksonville, 1999).

<u>World Book Encyclopedia</u>, 1985 ed., s.v. "Automation."

<u>World Book Encyclopedia</u>, 1985 ed., s.v. "Automobile.

www.ingramcontent.com/pod-product-compliance
Lightning Source LLC
Chambersburg PA
CBHW061431040426
42450CB00007B/991